CASE STUDY
RESEARCH
IN EDUCATION

Sharan B. Merriam

CASE STUDY RESEARCH IN EDUCATION

A Qualitative Approach

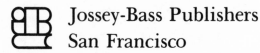 Jossey-Bass Publishers
San Francisco

CASE STUDY RESEARCH IN EDUCATION
A Qualitative Approach
by Sharan B. Merriam

Copyright © 1988 by: Jossey-Bass Inc., Publishers
350 Sansome Street
San Francisco, California 94104

Library of Congress Cataloging-in-Publication Data

Merriam, Sharan B.
  Case study research in education.

  (The Jossey-Bass education series) (The Jossey-Bass
higher education series) (The Jossey-Bass social and
behavioral science series)
  Bibliography: p.
  Includes index.
  1. Education—Research—Methodology. 2. Education—
Research—Case studies. 3. Case method. I. Title.
II. Series. III. Series: Jossey-Bass higher education
series. IV. Series: Jossey-Bass social and behavioral
science series.
LB1028.M396   1988   370'.7'8   88-42795
ISBN 1-55542-108-3 (alk. paper)
ISBN 1-55542-359-0 (paperback)
Manufactured in the United States of America

 The paper used in this book is acid-free and meets the
State of California requirements for recycled paper
(50 percent recycled waste, including 10 percent
postconsumer waste), which are the strictest guidelines
for recycled paper currently in use in the United States.

JACKET AND COVER DESIGN BY WILLI BAUM

FIRST EDITION
HB Printing   10 9 8 7 6 5 4 3
Code 8839

PB Printing   10 9 8 7 6 5 4 3
Code 9165

A joint publication in

THE JOSSEY-BASS EDUCATION SERIES

THE JOSSEY-BASS
HIGHER EDUCATION SERIES

THE JOSSEY-BASS
SOCIAL AND BEHAVIORAL SCIENCE SERIES

CONTENTS

Case Study Data**   119

8. The Components of Data Analysis   123

9. Using Special Techniques and Computers to
    Analyze Qualitative Data   147

10. Dealing with Validity, Reliability, and Ethics
    in Case Study Research   163

11. Writing the Case Study Report   185

    References   207

    Index   221

PREFACE

Case study research is nothing new. Historically, significant "cases" are part of the disciplines of medicine and law, and case studies have long been important in the development of other fields such as anthropology, psychology, sociology, management, social work, and political science. Recently education has turned to case study research to explore the processes and dynamics of practice. This type of research received considerable support and recognition in the late 1960s and early 1970s when the federal government funded in-depth studies of school integration, innovative science curriculum, the New Math, and so on. Such studies offered useful insights into educational practice and proved helpful in forming policy. In education as well as other areas of social practice, case study is a legitimate methodological option for researchers to consider when designing a study.

Material on case study as a research strategy can be found everywhere and nowhere. Since case study is an accepted research design in many disciplines, articles on methodology and actual case study reports do exist in journals and texts. This material is scattered across so many fields of study, however, that an educator with a special interest or methodological question may find it hard to locate information about case study research. Even within the field of education itself, information is widely dispersed in journal articles, research reports, conference proceedings, and general research texts.

Indeed, educators whose questions mandate a case study approach are handicapped by the lack of readily accessible materials and the lack of training in this method. Most basic research courses do not deal with the case study in any substantive way. Those interested in this approach must find someone with expertise in the method who can tutor them in its usage, or they must study materials related to the method. As noted, however, these materials are scattered. *Case Study Research in Education* was born out of this author's personal frustration with trying to find appropriate materials for doing, learning, and teaching about case study research in an educational setting. The book gathers together—in one place—pertinent information on case study as a research method and its application to questions of educational practice.

Although most educators have encountered case studies in their graduate school preparation or in their work setting, there is little precision in the use of the term *case study*. To some extent, case study has become a catchall category for studies that are not clearly experimental, survey, or historical. Further confusion stems from the fact that case study has been used interchangeably with fieldwork, ethnography, participant observation, exploratory research, and naturalistic inquiry. Moreover, case study does not equate with casework, case method, and case history. One of the two major purposes of this book is to delineate just what a case study *is* and, in particular, what a *qualitative* case study is. My second objective is to present the mechanics of conducting a case study in a simple, straightforward manner—including designing the study, collecting and analyzing data, and writing the case report.

I have focused on the qualitative case study because most case studies in education approach a problem of practice from a holistic perspective. That is, investigators use a case study design in order to gain an in-depth understanding of the situation and its meaning for those involved. The interest is in process rather than outcomes, in context rather than a specific variable, in discovery rather than confirmation. Such insights into aspects of educational practice can have a direct influence on policy, practice, and future research. The focus of this book, then, is on case studies that draw from what is commonly known as the qualitative research paradigm, rather than a quantitative, positivistic, experimental orientation. Thus this book can also serve as a reference on qualitative methods. Chapters on data collection techniques, data analysis, and concerns of reliability, validity, and ethics are germane to all forms of qualitative research. What distinguishes this book from others on qualitative methods is the use of qualitative data collection and analysis techniques in the service of a specific genre of research—the case study.

The qualitative case study is a particularly suitable methodology for dealing with critical problems of practice and extending the knowledge base of various aspects of education. Thoughtful counselors, administrators, and instructors are vitally interested in the questions that emerge in their daily work life. A case study approach is often the best methodology for addressing these problems in which understanding is sought in order to improve practice. This book has been written to allow educators to design and carry out a problem-centered, situation-specific, qualitative case study. The book is meant to be more than a how-to manual for conducting case study research, however. It has also been written to clarify the nature of case study research and, in particular, qualitative case study research. The intended audiences for this book, then, are teachers, researchers, and graduate students in education who are interested in the qualitative case study as a research option.

Overview of the Contents

The organization of the following chapters reflects, in general, the steps of a research investigation. Part One contains four chapters on the nature of qualitative case study research, types and uses of case studies, selecting the case to be investigated, and the place of theory and literature in case study research. Part Two consists of three chapters on collecting qualitative data from interviews, observations, and documents. The four chapters in Part Three deal with analyzing the data collected, handling the concerns of reliability, validity, and ethics, and writing the case report.

As already noted, *case study* is used by many people in

many different ways to mean many different things. The purpose of Chapter One is to differentiate case study from other
approaches to a research problem. A qualitative case study is an
intensive, holistic description and analysis of a bounded phenomenon such as a program, an institution, a person, a process,
or a social unit. The defining characteristics of a case study are
discussed in Chapter One, as are the philosophical assumptions
of qualitative research that underlie a qualitative case study.

Most case studies in education draw from other disciplines for both theory and method. Chapter Two explains how
concepts, theories, and techniques from anthropology, history,
sociology, and psychology in particular have influenced case
studies in education. Irrespective of disciplinary orientation,
case studies can also be described in terms of the end product—
a descriptive narrative, an interpretive account, or an evaluation. This chapter also explains when to select a case study design and points out its strengths and limitations.

Not everyone will have confidence in a case study design.
Chapter Three begins with a discussion of the characteristics
and skills needed to conduct a qualitative case study investigation. Once a person determines that he or she is suited to doing
this type of research, the individual must then define and select
the case. The chapter also explains how to select a sample of
people, events, or incidents within the case for intensive study.

Knowledge of previous research and theory can help one
to focus on the problem of interest and select the unit of analysis most relevant to the problem. Chapter Four explores the role
of theory and the place of the literature review in qualitative
case study research.

Chapters Five, Six, and Seven examine the three primary
means of collecting data in case study research. Interviews, discussed in Chapter Five, can range in structure from a list of predetermined questions to a totally free-ranging interview in
which nothing is set ahead of time. The success of an interview
depends on the nature of the interaction between the interviewer and respondent and on the interviewer's skill in asking
good questions. How to record and evaluate interview data is
also covered in Chapter Five. Observations differ from inter-

views in that the researcher obtains a firsthand account of the phenomenon of interest rather than relying on someone else's interpretation. Chapter Six discusses what to observe, the interdependent relationship between observer and observed, and how to record observations in the form of field notes. Chapter Seven presents the third primary source of case study data: documents. The term *document* is broadly defined to cover an assortment of written records, physical traces, and artifacts. Although some might be developed at the investigator's request, most are produced independently of the research study and thus offer a valuable resource for confirming insights gained through interviews and observations. Chapter Seven covers various types of documents, their use in case study research, and their strengths and limitations as a source of data.

Most texts on qualitative research and materials on case study research devote more space to theoretical discussions of methodology and data collection than to analyzing the data once they have been collected. This book redresses that imbalance with two full chapters on data analysis. Chapter Eight presents strategies for analyzing data *while* they are being collected. Intensive analysis begins after all the data have been gathered and presumes that all the information has been organized into a case study data base or case record. Several levels of analysis are possible—ranging from developing a descriptive account of the findings to developing categories, themes, or other concepts that interpret the meaning of the data in more abstract terms. Finally, one can build theory to explain the relationships among concepts and tentative hypotheses. Chapter Nine, also on data analysis, presents twelve specific strategies for deriving meaning from case study data and explains how to conduct a cross-case analysis. One section of Chapter Nine is devoted to the use of computers in analyzing qualitative data.

All researchers are concerned with producing findings that are reliable and valid. Chapter Ten explores the issues of validity and reliability in qualitative case study research. In particular, internal validity, reliability, and external validity are discussed and strategies are offered for dealing with each of these issues. Also of concern to researchers is how to conduct an investigation in an ethical manner. Chapter Ten closes with a section on ethics, paying particular attention to ethical dilemmas likely to arise in qualitative case study research.

Many an educator has been able to conceptualize a study, collect relevant data, analyze the data, and then fail to carry through in the important last step—writing up the results. Without this step, the research has little chance of advancing the knowledge base of education or having an impact on practice. Chapter Eleven is designed to help case study researchers complete the research process by writing a report of the investigation. The first half of the chapter offers suggestions for organizing the writing process—compiling the case record, determining the audience for the report, settling on the main message, and outlining the overall report. The rest of Chapter Eleven focuses on the *content* of the case report—its components and where to place them, how to achieve a good balance between description and analysis, and how to disseminate the study's findings.

Acknowledgments

The major impetus for this book came from my graduate students at Northern Illinois University and the University of Georgia who wanted to do a case study for their doctoral dissertation. Together we gathered materials and taught ourselves how to define a case, how to do a case study, and how to present the findings in a manner acceptable to august dissertation committees. My desire to be a better mentor in this process led to much reading and discussion with colleagues and to doing some case study research myself. An article on case study research that I published in *The Journal of Educational Thought* resulted in more thinking about this topic. It was also becoming clear that the stack of case study materials in the corner of my office needed some organization and interpretation to be helpful to students and others; hence, the draft of a book began to emerge.

As all authors know, there is nothing like trying to write a book to force clear thought on a topic. There is also no substitute for the help colleagues can give. Three colleagues of mine—

Ronald Cervero and Judith Goetz here at Georgia and Arlene Fingeret at North Carolina State—offered invaluable comments, insights, and suggestions on early draft chapters. Two other people also put many hours into this project. Catherine Zeph spent a large portion of her Kellogg doctoral assistantship reading and rereading the manuscript with red pen in one hand and Jossey-Bass editing guidelines in the other. Beverly Massey cheerfully and conscientiously moved files from disk to disk, typed, coordinated, and collated hundreds of pages of manuscript despite her many other responsibilities. To Beverly and Cathy, my sincere appreciation. Finally, I want to thank colleagues, family members, and friends for suffering through the process with me in the hope that life would eventually return to normal.

Athens, Georgia   Sharan B. Merriam
July 1988

THE AUTHOR

Sharan B. Merriam is professor of adult and continuing education at the University of Georgia in Athens, where her responsibilities include developing a research program under a Kellogg Foundation grant in continuing education and lifelong learning. She received her B.A. degree (1965) in English literature from Drew University, her M.Ed. degree (1971) in English education from Ohio University, and her Ed.D. degree (1978) in adult education from Rutgers University. Before coming to the University of Georgia, she served on the faculties of Northern Illinois University and Virginia Polytechnic Institute and State University.

Merriam's main research and writing activities have focused on adult education, adult development and learning, and qualitative research methods. She has served on steering committees for the annual North American Adult Education Research Conference and the Commission of Professors of Adult Education, chaired the 1984 Midwest Research-to-Practice Conference, and is an active member of the American Association for Adult and Continuing Education (AAACE) and the Postsecondary Division of the American Educational Research Association. She is currently coeditor of the *1990 Handbook of Adult and Continuing Education.* Her other books include *Philosophical Foundations of Adult Education* (with J. Elias, 1980), *Coping with Male Mid-life: A Systematic Analysis Using Literature as a Data Source* (1980), *Adult Education: Foundations of Practice* (with G. Darkenwald, 1982), winner of the 1985 Cyril O. Houle World Award for Literature in Adult Education, *Themes of Adulthood*

Through Literature (1983), *A Guide to Research for Educators and Trainers of Adults* (with E. L. Simpson, 1984), winner of the 1984 Phillip E. Frandson Memorial Award for Literature in Continuing Education, *Selected Writings on Philosophy and Adult Education* (editor, 1984), and *Adult Development: Implications for Adult Education* (1985).

CASE STUDY
RESEARCH
IN EDUCATION

PART ONE

FOUNDATIONS
OF QUALITATIVE
CASE STUDY RESEARCH

Few areas of practice offer as many opportunities for research as does the field of education. To begin with, education is a familiar arena. Potential researchers have had personal experience with formal schooling, at least through college, and everyone has learned in informal ways throughout their lives. Having an interest in knowing more about the field and in improving the practice of education leads to asking researchable questions, some of which are best approached through a case study research design.

Though the term *case study* is familiar to most people, there is little agreement on just what constitutes case study research. Cronbach (1982), for example, says that "all social scientists are engaged in case studies" in the sense that observations, whether in an annual census or of an individual, "take meaning from their time and place, and from the conceptions held by those who pose the questions and decide how to tabulate" (p. 75). That is, all research should take account of the context and also the relevant forces outside the unit being studied. Case study research, and in particular qualitative case study, is an ideal design for understanding and interpreting observations of educational phenomena.

Part One of this book provides the conceptual foundation for doing this type of research. Case study as a research design is first delineated from other research designs and then defined. Types and uses of case studies are discussed, as are the design's strengths and limitations. Other topics covered in the first four chapters deal with determining whether one is suited for this type of research, how to select a case and a sample within the case for intensive study, how theory functions in a case study, and how to approach previous research and writing on the subject of interest.

Case study is a basic design that can accommodate a variety of disciplinary perspectives, as well as philosophical perspectives on the nature of research itself. A case study can test theory or build theory, incorporate random or purposive sampling, and include quantitative and qualitative data. There is considerable debate among researchers, however, about the extent to which traditional methods of data collection and analysis can be used in conjunction with qualitative methods in a research study. "Pragmatists see a more instrumental relationship between paradigm and methods" (Firestone, 1987, p. 16) and call for an end to the battle of qualitative versus quantitative methods (Reichardt and Cook, 1979) or have simply combined methods and left the philosophical battle to others (Smith and Louis, 1982; Miles and Huberman, 1984). Guba (1987) suggests separating methods from paradigm: "One can use both quantitative and qualitative techniques in combination whether the paradigm of orientation is . . . naturalistic or traditional." However, "*no* possibility exists that there can be an accommodation at the paradigm level" (p. 31). Kidder and Fine (1987, p. 72) concur, noting that there is nothing mysterious about combining quantitative and qualitative measures. This is, in fact, a form of triangulation that enhances the validity and reliability of one's study. But "troubling problems arise" when one is trying to reach conclusions across studies conducted from different paradigms.

From a purist position, method and paradigm are inextricably linked. Smith and Heshusius (1986, p. 9) write that "if one extends the different sets of assumptions to their logical implications, it is clear the two perspectives part company over major issues such as the conceptualization given such basic conditions as validity and reliability, the place of techniques in the inquiry process, and the interpretation of research results." Firestone (1987, p. 16), in comparing the rhetoric of a qualitative and quantitative study of the same research problem, found that each used "different techniques of presentation to project divergent assumptions about the world and different means to persuade the reader of its conclusions." All aspects of a research inquiry thus appear to be logically connected to the paradigm of choice.

In this book, case study research is defined and described from the perspective of the qualitative or naturalistic research paradigm, which, in this author's opinion, defines the methods and techniques most suitable for collecting and analyzing data. I chose this paradigm because I believe that research focused on discovery, insight, and understanding from the perspectives of those being studied offers the greatest promise of making significant contributions to the knowledge base and practice of education. Furthermore, most case studies in education are qualitative and hypothesis-generating, rather than quantitative and hypothesis-testing, studies. Naturalistic inquiry, which focuses on meaning in context, requires a data collection instrument sensitive to underlying meaning when gathering and interpreting data. Humans are best-suited for this task—and best when using methods that make use of human sensibilities such as interviewing, observing, and analyzing. Nonprobability forms of sampling and inductive data analysis are consistent with the goals and assumptions of this paradigm, as are specific ways of ensuring for validity and reliability.

The four chapters that comprise Part One of this book thus locate case study research within the qualitative research paradigm. The philosophical assumptions underlying qualitative research are presented in Chapter One. Although occasional reference is made to a conventional, quantitative paradigm for comparison, the discussions in Part One on the research prob-

lem, sampling, theory, and literature in case study research reflect a qualitative focus. The chapters in Part One thus lay the
foundation for understanding the nature of qualitative case study
research and pave the way for subsequent chapters that focus
on case study research itself.

CHAPTER 1

The Case Study Approach
to Research Problems

Most teachers, graduate students, and researchers in education and other applied social sciences have encountered case studies in their training or work. But while many have heard of case study research, there is little consensus on what constitutes a case study or how one actually goes about doing this type of research. Some of the confusion stems from the fact that various sources equate case study research with fieldwork, ethnography, participant observation, qualitative research, naturalistic inquiry, grounded theory, exploratory research, phenomenology, and hypothesis generation. The terms *case history, case record,* and *case method,* sometimes used in conjunction with case study, further confuse the issue, as do questions related to the case study's purposes, goals, and functions. Procedural confusion arises from questions about the type of data that can be used in a case study, how best to collect the data, and how to interpret them.

This chapter presents case study—and, in particular, *qualitative* case study—as a research design in its own right, one that can be distinguished from other approaches to a research problem. Discussion of the distinguishing characteristics of a qualitative case study is followed by an examination of the philosophical assumptions associated with qualitative research in general.

Case Study as a Research Design

Every discipline depends on research activity to expand its knowledge base. Applied areas such as education, counseling, administration, social work, and medicine also value research as a means of understanding, informing, and improving practice. Typically, the practitioner becomes aware of an event or situation that is problematic. The puzzling situation can be dealt with in several informal ways: the practitioner could ask a friend how he or she handled a similar situation, could read an article or book that might prove helpful, or could deal directly with the situation by using a trial-and-error approach. A more systematic approach, and probably more expedient in the long run, would be to design an investigation of the problem—in effect, to do research. Broadly defined, research is systematic inquiry. There are numerous well-tested designs and techniques to help guide the inquiry. Case study is one such research design that can be used to study a phenomenon systematically.

A research design is similar to an architectural blueprint. It is a plan for assembling, organizing, and integrating information (data), and it results in a specific end product (research findings). The selection of a particular design is determined by how the problem is shaped, by the questions it raises, and by the type of end product desired.

The most basic distinction in design is between experimental and nonexperimental. Experimental research assumes that the researcher can manipulate the variables of interest—that is, there is a great deal of control over the research situation. Experimental research is also characterized by its major intent: to investigate cause-and-effect relationships. In order to determine cause and effect, it is essential to assign subjects at random to experimental and control groups. In most educational situations, however, it is not possible to control all the variables of interest. Thus in education, as in other applied fields, cause and effect is studied through one of two variations of a true experimental design. In a quasi-experimental study, control is maintained to the extent possible and randomization is approximated through statistical and other procedures. The second variation on a true experimental design is ex post facto research in which one is interested in conditions that *might* have caused an effect, but these conditions have already occurred. The investigator arrives "after the fact" (ex post facto) and tries to determine causal relationships. Studies linking cancer to smoking are ex post facto.

Nonexperimental or, as it is often called, *descriptive* research is undertaken when description and explanation (rather than prediction based on cause and effect) are sought, when it is not possible or feasible to manipulate the potential causes of behavior, and when variables are not easily identified or are too embedded in the phenomenon to be extracted for study. The aim of descriptive research is to examine events or phenomena. "The purpose of most descriptive research is limited to characterizing something as it is, though some descriptive research suggests tentative causal relationships. There is no manipulation of treatments or subjects; the researcher takes things as they are" (McMillan and Schumacher, 1984, p. 26). Survey research, historical research, and case studies are forms of descriptive, nonexperimental research.

Survey research typically assesses a few variables across a large number of instances, whereas a case study concentrates on many, if not all, the variables present in a single unit. Survey research is deductive in nature—that is, variables are selected for investigation from a theory or conceptual model before the study. Hypotheses about the extent, nature, frequency, and relationships among variables often guide this type of research. Findings are then presented quantitatively. Descriptive case studies, on the other hand, are usually inductive in nature. It is impossible to identify all the important variables ahead of time. Results are presented qualitatively, using words and pictures rather than numbers.

It is important to distinguish between survey research as a genre and using a survey (that is, a questionnaire) to gather information. A survey is often used in quasi-experimental and ex post facto studies. A case study can also include data gathered by a survey instrument. For example, a case study investigation of an innovative high school science program may involve sending a questionnaire to parents asking their opinion of the program. Their responses would form part of the data base for the case study.

Historical research is essentially descriptive, and elements of historical research and case study often merge. Yin (1984) discusses the two approaches:

> Histories are the preferred strategy when there is virtually no access or control. Thus, the distinctive contribution of the historical method is in dealing with the "dead" past—that is, when no relevant persons are alive to report, even retrospectively, what occurred, and when an investigator must rely on primary documents, secondary documents, and cultural and physical artifacts as the main sources of evidence. Histories can, of course, be done about contemporary events; in this situation, the strategy begins to overlap with that of the case study.
>
> The case study is preferred in examining contemporary events, but when the relevant behaviors cannot be manipulated. Thus, the case study relies on many of the same techniques as a history, but it adds two sources of evidence not usually included in the historian's repertoire: direct observation and systematic interviewing. Again, although case studies and histories can overlap, the case study's unique strength is its ability to deal with a full variety of evidence—documents, artifacts, interviews, and observations [pp. 19–20].

An example of how historical research can be differentiated from a case study that is historical in nature might be as follows: A study of urban public schools in the late 1800s would rely primarily on public school records for data. A case study of an urban school in the 1960s would use public documents, as well, but it might also make use of television or videotaped reports and interviews of persons who had been directly associated with the case.

In summary, then, the decision to choose an experimental design or some variation of it, or a nonexperimental research design such as a case study, depends on consideration of the following points:

1. *The nature of the research questions:* "What" and "how many" are best answered by survey research. "How" and "why" questions are appropriate for case study, history, and experimental designs (Yin, 1984).
2. *The amount of control:* The more control one has, the more "experimental" the design. The least amount of control characterizes historical research, since no treatment is manipulated and no observations are made.
3. *The desired end product:* This factor is linked to the nature of the questions asked. Will the results be presented as the end product of a cause-and-effect investigation? Will the end product be a holistic, intensive description and interpretation of a contemporary phenomenon? Or quantification of the extent and nature of certain variables with a population? Or a historical analysis? These questions come into play when one attempts to select the most appropriate research design.

Case Study Defined

The nature of the research questions, the amount of control, and the desired end product are issues to be considered when deciding whether case study is the most appropriate design for investigating the problem of interest. A fourth and probably deciding factor is whether a *bounded system* (Smith, 1978) can be identified as the focus of the investigation. That is, a case study is an examination of a specific phenomenon such as a program, an event, a person, a process, an institution, or a social group. The bounded system, or case, might be selected because it is an instance of some concern, issue, or hypothesis. It would be, in Adelman, Jenkins, and Kemmis's (1983, p. 3) words, *"an instance drawn from a class."* If the researcher is interested in the process of mainstreaming children into regular classes, for example, he or she would select a particular instance of mainstreaming to study in depth. An instance could be an individual child, a specific program, or a school. A case might also be selected because it is itself intrinsically interesting, and one would study it to achieve as full an understanding of the phenomenon as possible. Choosing to study a college counseling program for returning adult students is an example of selecting a case for its intrinsic interest. In both situations, the mainstreaming process and the counseling program, the case is identified as a bounded system. "The most straightforward examples of 'bounded systems' are those in which the boundaries have a common sense obviousness, e.g. an individual teacher, a single school, or perhaps an innovatory programme" (Adelman, Jenkins, and Kemmis, 1983, p. 3).

Unlike experimental, survey, or historical research, case study does not claim any particular methods for data collection or data analysis. Any and all methods of gathering data from testing to interviewing can be used in a case study, although certain techniques are used more than others. Since this book focuses on case studies that are *qualitative* in nature, data gathering and analysis techniques characteristic of qualitative research are emphasized. The decision to focus on qualitative case studies stems from the fact that this design is chosen precisely because researchers are interested in insight, discovery, and interpretation rather than hypothesis testing. Case study has in fact been differentiated from other research designs by what Cronbach (1975, p. 123) calls "interpretation in context." By concentrating on a single phenomenon or entity ("the case"), this approach aims to uncover the interaction of significant factors characteristic of the phenomenon. The case study seeks holistic description and explanation. As Yin (1984) observes, case study is a design particularly suited to situations where it is impossible to separate the phenomenon's variables from their context.

Several writers have advanced definitions of the case

study congruent with this discussion. Wilson (1979, p. 448), for example, conceptualizes the case study as a process "which tries to describe and analyze some entity in qualitative, complex and comprehensive terms not infrequently as it unfolds over a period of time." MacDonald and Walker's (1977, p. 181) definition of a case study as "the examination of an instance in action" is congruent with Guba and Lincoln's (1981, p. 371) statement that the purpose is "to reveal the properties of the class to which the instance being studied belongs." Becker (1968, p. 233) defines the purposes of a case study as twofold: "to arrive at a comprehensive understanding of the groups under study" and "to develop general theoretical statements about regularities in social structure and process."

The case study can be further defined by its special features. Table 1 lists several case study characteristics from five separate sources. While the number of characteristics and the terminology may differ from source to source, a review of these and other writings suggests that the following four characteristics are essential properties of a qualitative case study: particularistic, descriptive, heuristic, and inductive.

Particularistic means that case studies focus on a particular situation, event, program, or phenomenon. The case itself is important for what it reveals about the phenomenon and for what it might represent. This specificity of focus makes it an especially good design for practical problems—for questions, situations, or puzzling occurrences arising from everyday practice. Case studies "concentrate attention on the way particular groups of people confront specific problems, taking a holistic view of the situation. They are problem centered, small scale, entrepreneurial endeavors" (Shaw, 1978, p. 2).

Descriptive means that the end product of a case study is a rich, "thick" description of the phenomenon under study. *Thick description* is a term from anthropology and means the complete, literal description of the incident or entity being investigated. It also means "interpreting the meaning of . . . demographic and descriptive data in terms of cultural norms and mores, community values, deep-seated attitudes and notions, and the like" (Guba and Lincoln, 1981, p. 119). Case studies in-

Table 1. Characteristics of Qualitative Case Studies.

Guba and Lincoln (1981)	Helmstadter (1970)	Hoaglin and Others (1982)	Stake (1981)	Wilson (1979)
• "thick" description	• can be used to remedy or improve practice	• specificity	• inductive	• particularistic
• grounded	• results are hypotheses	• description of parties and motives	• multiplicity of data	• holistic
• holistic and lifelike	• design is flexible	• description of key issues	• descriptive	• longitudinal
• conversation-style format	• can be applied to troubled situations	• can suggest solutions	• specific	• qualitative
• illuminates meaning			• heuristic	
• builds on tacit knowledge				

clude as many variables as possible and portray their interaction, often over a period of time. Case studies can thus be longitudinal. They have also been labeled "holistic," "lifelike," "grounded," and "exploratory." The description is usually qualitative—that is, instead of reporting findings in numerical data, "case studies use prose and literary techniques to describe, elicit images, and analyze situations. . . . They present documentation of events, quotes, samples and artifacts" (Wilson, 1979, p. 448).

Heuristic means that case studies illuminate the reader's understanding of the phenomenon under study. They can bring about the discovery of new meaning, extend the reader's experience, or confirm what is known. "Previously unknown relationships and variables can be expected to emerge from case studies leading to a rethinking of the phenomenon being studied. Insights into how things get to be the way they are can be expected to result from case studies" (Stake, 1981, p. 47).

Inductive means that, for the most part, case studies rely on inductive reasoning. Generalizations, concepts, or hypotheses emerge from an examination of data—data grounded in the context itself. Occasionally one may have tentative working hypotheses at the outset of a case study, but these expectations are subject to reformulation as the study proceeds. Discovery of new relationships, concepts, and understanding, rather than verification or predetermined hypotheses, characterizes qualitative case studies.

Olson (in Hoaglin and others, 1982, pp. 138–139) has developed a list of case study characteristics that may illuminate the nature of this research design. These "aspects," as she refers to them, can be loosely grouped under three of the major characteristics just discussed. Three statements reflect the case study's *particularistic* nature:

- It can suggest to the reader what to do or what not to do in a similar situation.
- It can examine a specific instance but illuminate a general problem.
- It may or may not be influenced by the author's bias.

Several aspects of a case study listed by Olson address its *descriptive* nature:

- It can illustrate the complexities of a situation—the fact that not one but many factors contributed to it.
- It has the advantage of hindsight yet can be relevant in the present.
- It can show the influence of personalities on the issue.
- It can show the influence of the passage of time on the issue —deadlines, change of legislators, cessation of funding, and so on.
- It can include vivid material—quotations, interviews, newspaper articles, and so on.
- It can obtain information from a wide variety of sources.
- It can cover many years and describe how the preceding decades led to a situation.
- It can spell out differences of opinion on the issue and suggest how these differences have influenced the result.
- It can present information in a wide variety of ways . . . and from the viewpoints of different groups.

The *heuristic* quality of a case study is suggested by these aspects:

- It can explain the reasons for a problem, the background of a situation, what happened, and why.
- It can explain why an innovation worked or failed to work.
- It can discuss and evaluate alternatives not chosen.
- It can evaluate, summarize, and conclude, thus increasing its potential applicability.

Attempts to define case study often center on delineating what is unique about the research design. As mentioned earlier, the uniqueness of a case study lies not so much in the methods employed (although these are important) as in the questions asked and their relationship to the end product. Stake (1981) takes this notion one step further and claims that knowledge learned from case study is different from other research knowledge in four important ways. Case study knowledge is:

- More concrete—case study knowledge resonates with our own experience because it is more vivid, concrete, and sensory than abstract.
- More contextual—our experiences are rooted in context, as is knowledge in case studies. This knowledge is distinguishable from the abstract, formal knowledge derived from other research designs.
- More developed by reader interpretation—readers bring to a case study their own experience and understanding, which lead to generalizations when new data for the case are added to old data. Stake considers these generalizations to be "part of the knowledge produced by case studies" (p. 36).
- Based more on reference populations determined by the reader—in generalizing as described above, readers have some population in mind. Thus, unlike traditional research, the reader participates in extending generalization to reference populations (Stake, 1981, pp. 35–36).

In defining a phenomenon such as a case study, it is often helpful to point out what it is *not*. Case study research is not the same as casework, case method, case history, or case record. *Casework* denotes "the developmental, adjustment, remedial, or corrective procedures that appropriately follow diagnosis of the causes of maladjustment" (Good and Scates, 1954, p. 729). *Case method* is an instructional technique whereby the major ingredients of a case study are presented to students for illustrative purposes or problem-solving experiences. Case studies as teaching devices have become very popular in law, medicine, and business. "For teaching purposes, a case study need not reflect a complete or accurate rendition of actual events; rather, its purpose is to establish a framework for discussion and debate among students" (Yin, 1984, p. 14). *Case history*, the tracing of a person, group, or institution's past, is sometimes part of a case study. In medicine and social work, case histories (also called *case records)* are used in much the same sense as casework—to facilitate service to the client.

In summary, then, the qualitative case study can be defined as an intensive, holistic description and analysis of a single entity, phenomenon, or social unit. Case studies are particularistic, descriptive, and heuristic and rely heavily on inductive reasoning in handling multiple data sources. The nature of this particular research design is inextricably linked to certain philosophical assumptions. In the following section, theoretical underpinnings of the qualitative case study are discussed.

Philosophical Assumptions

With few exceptions, discussions of case study are embedded in the growing body of literature on qualitative research and naturalistic inquiry. That is not to imply that qualitative research equals a case study or that one cannot use quantitative data in a case study. Rather, the logic of this type of research derives from the worldview of qualitative research. Within qualitative research there are numerous traditions from anthropology, psychology, and sociology, each having internally consistent assumptions about human nature and society, appropriate foci of study, and methodology (Jacob, 1987, 1988). Overall, however, in a qualitative approach to research the paramount objective is to understand the *meaning* of an experience. In contrast to quantitative research, which takes apart a phenomenon to examine component parts (which become the variables of the study), qualitative research strives to understand how all the parts work together to form a whole. "It is an effort," Patton writes,

> to understand situations in their uniqueness as part of a particular context and the interactions there. This understanding is an end in itself, so that it is not attempting to predict what may happen in the future necessarily, but to understand the nature of that setting—what it means for participants to be in that setting, what their lives are like, what's going

> on for them, what their meanings are, what the
> world looks like in that particular setting—and in
> the analysis to be able to communicate that faith-
> fully to others who are interested in that setting.
> ... The analysis strives for depth of understanding
> [Patton, 1985, p. 1].

Qualitative research has most often been presented in contrast to the "traditional" or "scientific" paradigm, which depends upon a very different view of the world. Traditional research is based on the assumption that there is a single, objective reality—the world out there—that we can observe, know, and measure. Facts have been amassed by scientists to describe the world, and in some instances laws have been advanced to explain certain aspects of this reality. From a research perspective, this worldview holds the nature of reality to be constant. Confirmation of what is out there is desired; research is focused on outcomes; reliability of measurement is stressed.

In contrast, qualitative research assumes that there are multiple realities—that the world is not an objective thing out there but a function of personal interaction and perception. It is a highly subjective phenomenon in need of interpreting rather than measuring. Beliefs rather than facts form the basis of perception. Research is exploratory, inductive, and emphasizes processes rather than ends. In this paradigm, there are no predetermined hypotheses, no treatments, and no restrictions on the end product. One does not manipulate variables or administer a treatment. What one *does* do is observe, intuit, sense what is occurring in a natural setting—hence the term *naturalistic* inquiry. Thus these are just several of the contrasting elements of qualitative and quantitative research paradigms—some of the major distinctions gleaned from thorough discussions in Bogdan and Biklen (1982), Guba (1978), Reichardt and Cook (1979), Owens (1982), and Leininger (1985).

The list presented in Table 2, while not exhaustive, does differentiate these two orientations to research. Several characteristics of qualitative research are worth stressing, for they figure prominently in case study research. First, qualitative re-

Table 2. Characteristics of Qualitative and Quantitative Research.

Point of Comparison	Qualitative Research	Quantitative Research
Focus of research	Quality (nature, essence)	Quantity (how much, how many)
Philosophical roots	Phenomenology, symbolic interaction	Positivism, logical empiricism
Associated phrases	Fieldwork, ethnographic, naturalistic, grounded, subjective	Experimental, empirical, statistical
Goal of investigation	Understanding, description, discovery, hypothesis generating	Prediction, control, description, confirmation, hypothesis testing
Design characteristics	Flexible, evolving, emergent	Predetermined, structured
Setting	Natural, familiar	Unfamiliar, artificial
Sample	Small, nonrandom, theoretical	Large, random, representative
Data collection	Researcher as primary instrument, interviews, observations	Inanimate instruments (scales, tests, surveys, questionnaires, computers)
Mode of analysis	Inductive (by researcher)	Deductive (by statistical methods)
Findings	Comprehensive, holistic, expansive	Precise, narrow, reductionist

searchers are primarily concerned with *process* rather than outcomes or products. How do certain things happen? What is the "natural" history of the activity or event under study? What happens with the passage of time? Second, qualitative researchers are interested in *meaning*—how people make sense of their lives, what they experience, how they interpret these experiences, how they structure their social worlds. It is assumed that meaning is embedded in people's experiences and mediated through the investigator's own perceptions. A researcher cannot get "outside" the phenomenon.

Third, the importance of the researcher in qualitative case study cannot be overemphasized. The researcher is the *primary instrument* for data collection and analysis. Data are mediated through this human instrument, the researcher, rather than through some inanimate inventory, questionnaire, or machine. Certain characteristics differentiate the human researcher from other data collection instruments: The researcher as instrument is responsive to the context; he or she can adapt techniques to the circumstances; the total context can be considered; what is known about the situation can be expanded through sensitivity to nonverbal aspects; the human instrument can process data immediately, can clarify and summarize as the study evolves, and can explore anomalous responses (Guba and Lincoln, 1981).

A fourth characteristic of qualitative research is that it usually involves *fieldwork*. One must physically go to the people, setting, site, institution ("the field"), in order to observe behavior in its natural setting. This is customarily done by anthropologists whose interest is to learn about other cultures. Most investigations that describe and interpret a social unit or process, as in case studies, necessitate becoming intimately familiar with the phenomenon being studied. Some specialized types of case studies such as those built from medical records or census data may rely exclusively on written materials, but these are the exceptions.

Two other important aspects of qualitative research that distinguish it from quantitative work are qualitative *description* and *induction*. In qualitative research one is interested in process, meaning, and understanding. Words or pictures rather than numbers are used to convey what the researcher has learned about the phenomenon. Qualitative research is thus descriptive. Finally, qualitative research is largely inductive. This type of research builds abstractions, concepts, hypotheses, or theories, rather than testing existing theory. "Purely inductive research begins with collection of data—empirical observations or measurements of some kind—and builds theoretical categories and propositions from relationships discovered among data" (Goetz and LeCompte, 1984, p. 4). In contrast to deductive researchers who "hope to find data to match a theory, inductive researchers hope to find a theory that explains their data" (p. 4).

Another approach to examining the philosophical assumptions underlying case study is taken by Kenny and Grotelueschen (1980). It is not helpful, in their opinion, to position the case study vis-à-vis the qualitative/quantitative dichotomy because then the case study is not defined on its own merits or it becomes an "undefined 'dumping ground' for nontraditional studies of all kinds" (p. 9). The qualitative/quantitative debate may be spurious anyway because "quantities are *of* qualities, and a measured quality *has* the magnitude expressed in its measure" (Kaplan in Kenny and Grotelueschen, 1980, p. 29).

Kenny and Grotelueschen (1980) review how three philosophical orientations—phenomenology, hermeneutics, and theory of tacit knowledge—have been used to make a case for case study research. The qualitative research paradigm does draw heavily from these schools of thought, but building a philosophical rationale for case study from these philosophies results in "problems of incompleteness and internal consistency . . . which can result in implications and positions devastating to case study" (p. 11). The authors propose two alternative approaches for justifying case study—one pragmatic and the other historical. A *pragmatic* justification emphasizes the applied nature of case study research. As a method it can be advocated on grounds that it is more useful, more appropriate, more workable than other research designs for a given situation. Knowledge produced by case study would then be judged on the extent to which it is understandable and applicable—thus a pragmatic conception of truth undergirds this approach. A *historical* justification recognizes the longitudinal or latently historical nature of case studies. They suggest viewing case study "as historical explanation in situationally specific settings (i.e., cases)." Further, "historical documentation, interpretation, and explanation" can serve as a model for case study research (p. 41).

Whether one views the philosophical foundations of the case study from a pragmatic or historical perspective, or draws upon the qualitative paradigm, is not as important as reflecting on one's assumptions and making them explicit at the outset of a case study investigation. The selection of data-gathering techniques, the way one chooses to organize and interpret data, and notions of validity, reliability, and generalizability of one's findings hinge upon one's philosophical orientation. These aspects of case study research are discussed in more detail in the following chapters.

Summary

This chapter has delineated the nature of case study as a research design. A qualitative case study is an intensive, holistic description and analysis of a single instance, phenomenon, or social unit. The main concern of case studies versus surveys or experimental research is "interpretation in context" (Shaw, 1978, p. 13). Case studies are particularistic in that they focus on a specific situation or phenomenon; they are descriptive; and they are heuristic—that is, they offer insights into the phenomenon under study. Philosophical assumptions underlying the case study draw from the qualitative rather than the quantitative research paradigm. Qualitative inquiry is inductive—focusing on process, understanding, and interpretation—rather than deductive and experimental. This book, then, is oriented toward case study research that is qualitative in nature, emphasizing description and interpretation within a bounded context.

CHAPTER 2

Types and Uses
of Case Study Research
in Education

Case studies in education tend to draw from other disciplines for both theory and method. In particular, theory and technique from anthropology, sociology, psychology, and history have informed case study investigations in education. Case studies can also be differentiated in terms of their end product. Some are descriptive, others are interpretive, and still others are evaluative. This chapter explores how case studies in education draw from other disciplines and how they can be differentiated by whether they are primarily descriptive, interpretive, or evaluative. The second half of the chapter discusses when to use a case study design and evaluates the strengths and limitations of case study research.

The Influence of Other Disciplines

Certain fields of study use case study research for specific purposes. Law, medicine, psychology, and social work, for example, often employ case studies on behalf of individual clients.

Political science, business, journalism, economics, and government have found case studies helpful in formulating policy. Case studies in *education* can focus on individual students—to diagnose learning problems, for example. They have also been used in the service of policy formation. More commonly, though, case study research in education seeks to understand specific issues and problems of practice. In so doing, case studies in education often draw upon other disciplines such as anthropology, history, sociology, and psychology both for theoretical orientation and for techniques of data collection and analysis.

Ethnography (from anthropology) is itself a research design developed by anthropologists to study human society and culture. Recently, the term *ethnography* has been used interchangeably with fieldwork, case study, qualitative research, and so on. For anthropologists, however, the term has two distinct meanings. Ethnography is a set of methods used to collect data, and it is the written record that is the product of using ethnographic techniques. Ethnographic techniques are the strategies researchers use to collect data about the social order, setting, or situation being investigated. Common techniques of data gathering are interviewing, documentary analysis, life history, investigator diaries, and participant observation. Just using these techniques, however, does not necessarily produce an ethnography in the second sense of the word. An ethnography is a sociocultural interpretation of the data. As analytic descriptions or reconstructions of participants' symbolic meanings and patterns of social interaction, "ethnographies recreate for the reader the shared beliefs, practices, artifacts, folk knowledge, and behaviors of some group of people" (Goetz and LeCompte, 1984, p. 2).

An *ethnographic case study*, then, is more than an intensive, holistic description and analysis of a social unit or phenomenon. It is a sociocultural analysis of the unit of study. Concern with the cultural context is what sets this type of study apart from other qualitative research. Wolcott (1980) distinguishes sharply between the techniques of ethnography and the ethnographic account itself: "Specific ethnographic techniques are freely available to any researcher who wants to approach a

problem or setting descriptively. It is the essential anthropological concern for cultural context that distinguishes ethnographic
method from fieldwork techniques and makes genuine ethnography distinct from other 'on-site-observer' approaches. And
when cultural interpretation is the goal, the ethnographer must
be thinking like an anthropologist, not just looking like one" (p.
59).

Goetz and LeCompte (1984, p. 22), in tracing the history
of educational ethnography from its roots in the first decades of
this century to the present day, note that "culture remains a
unifying construct of this tradition." Whatever the unit of study
—students, schools, learning, curriculum, informal education—
an ethnographic case study is characterized by its sociocultural
interpretation. An ethnographic case study of a junior high
school, for example, would take into account the community at
large and its cultural context. The history of the neighborhood,
social-economic factors, the community's racial and ethnic
makeup, the attitudes of parents, residents, and school officials
toward education—all would be important components of this
ethnographic case study.

A second type of case study found in education is the *historical case study.* Just as ethnographic case studies distinguish
between technique and account, so do historical case studies.
This type of research employs techniques common to historiog-
raphy—in particular, the use of primary source material. The
handling of historical material is systematic and involves learning to distinguish between primary and secondary sources. The
nature of the account also distinguishes this form of case study.
In applied fields such as education, historical case studies have
tended to be descriptions of institutions, programs, and practices as they have evolved in time. Historical case studies may
involve more than a chronological history of an event, however.
To understand an event and apply one's knowledge to present
practice means knowing the context of the event, the assumptions behind it, and perhaps the event's impact on the institution or participants.

Bogdan and Biklen (1982), in their discussion of types of
case study, list historical organizational case studies as one form

common in educational research. These studies focus on a specific organization and trace its development (p. 59). "One might do a study of a 'free school,' " for example, "tracing how it came into being, what its first year was like, what changes occurred over time, what it is like now (if it is still operating), or how it came to close (if it did)" (p. 59). The key to historical case studies, organizational or otherwise, is the notion of investigating the phenomenon over a period of time. One still wishes to present a holistic description and analysis of a specific phenomenon (the case), but from a historical perspective.

A third type of qualitative case study employs concepts, theories, and measurement techniques from psychology in investigating educational problems. The focus of a *psychological case study* is on the individual. The most famous precedent for case study in psychology was set by Freud in the early 1900s. His intensive self-analysis combined with case studies of a few individuals led to uncovering the unconscious life that is repressed but nevertheless governs behavior.

Psychologists investigating learning have had the most direct relevance to education. Again there are famous precedents for using case study to gain insight into learning processes. Ebbinghaus in the late nineteenth century, for example, self-administered thousands of tasks in the study of memory (Dukes, 1965). His findings provided the basis for memory research for the next half century. Piaget in studying his own children developed stages of cognitive structure that have had an enormous impact on curriculum and instruction. Indeed, his theory is still being tested and refined in educational research investigations. Finally, many studies in child and adult development have employed a qualitative case study as the mode of inquiry. Vaillant's (1977) findings about mental health are derived from longitudinal case studies of ninety-five Harvard men; Levinson studied forty men and built a theory of male adult development (Levinson, 1978).

The focus on the individual as a way to investigate some aspect of human behavior is what characterizes the psychological case study. In education a case study of an individual, program, event, or process might well be informed by a psychological concept. A case study of an elderly learner might draw upon Piaget's theory of cognitive development, for example, or research on behavior change might inform a case study of a patient education program.

Case studies in education might also draw upon theory and technique from sociology. Rather than focusing on an individual as in a psychological orientation, or on culture as in an anthropological study, *sociological case studies* attend to the constructs of society and socialization in studying educational phenomena. Sociologists are interested in demographics, social life and the roles people play in it, the community, social institutions such as the family, church, and government, classes of people including minority and economic groups, and social problems such as crime, racial prejudice, divorce, and mental illness. Educational case studies drawing upon sociology have explored such topics as student peer interaction as a function of high school social structure, the effect of role sets on teachers' interactions with students, the actual versus the hidden school curriculum, the relationship of schooling to equalities and inequalities in society at large, and so on (Goetz and LeCompte, 1984).

Until the 1960s, research methods in educational sociology were dominated by large-scale surveys, quantification, and experimentation (Bogdan and Biklen, 1982). By the 1970s, "sociologists had begun to address a gap in their knowledge base that had confounded efforts to explain intriguing correlations between classroom processes and other social phenomenon" (Goetz and LeCompte, 1984, p. 28). Qualitative approaches including case studies of the social life of schools and their participants began to appear. In 1967, sociologists Glaser and Strauss published *The Discovery of Grounded Theory,* a definitive work on how to build theory from descriptive data "grounded" in real-life situations. Several of the techniques for data collection and analysis—theoretical sampling and the constant comparative method in particular—are used by case study researchers and will be discussed more fully in subsequent chapters.

Thus sociology, like history, anthropology, and psychology, has influenced the theory and methods of case studies in education. What makes these case studies in *education* is their focus on questions, issues, and concerns broadly related to teaching and learning. The setting, delivery system, curriculum, student body, and theoretical orientation may vary widely, but the general arena of education remains central to these studies.

Descriptive, Interpretive, Evaluative Case Studies

Irrespective of disciplinary orientation or area of specific interest, case studies can also be described by the nature of the final report. Is the end product largely descriptive? Does it present an interpretation of the data? Is it an analysis? Does it build theory? Does it present judgments about the worth of a program? The end product of a case study can be primarily descriptive, interpretive, or evaluative.

A *descriptive* case study in education is one that presents a detailed account of the phenomenon under study—a historical case study that chronicles a sequence of events, for example. Lijphart (1971, p. 691) calls descriptive case studies "atheoretical." They are "entirely descriptive and move in a theoretical vacuum; they are neither guided by established or hypothesized generalizations nor motivated by a desire to formulate general hypotheses." They are useful, though, in presenting basic information about areas of education where little research has been conducted. Innovative programs and practices are often the focus of descriptive case studies in education. Such studies often form a data base for future comparison and theory building. Moore (1986), for example, conducted case studies of high school interns to find out how newcomers in organizations learn. He developed case studies of interns in such diverse settings as a furniture-making shop, an animal protection league, a hospital speech clinic, a food cooperative, a museum, and a labor union. With these descriptive studies he later devised a conceptual framework about learning in nonschool settings. Whatever the area of inquiry, basic description of the subject being studied comes before hypothesizing or theory testing.

Interpretive case studies, too, contain rich, thick description. These descriptive data, however, are used to develop conceptual categories or to illustrate, support, or challenge theoretical assumptions held prior to the data gathering. If there is a lack of theory, or if existing theory does not adequately explain the phenomenon, hypotheses cannot be developed to structure a research investigation. A case study researcher gathers as much information about the problem as possible with the intent of interpreting or theorizing about the phenomenon. A researcher might study how students come to an understanding of mathematical concepts, for example. Rather than just describing what was observed or what students reported in interviews, the investigator might take all the data and develop a typology, a continuum, or categories that conceptualize different approaches to the task. In another example, Medina (1987) studied the literacy-related activities of a rural farm family and interpreted the data in terms of the meaning of functional literacy in a rural context. The *level* of abstraction and conceptualization in interpretive case studies may range from suggesting relationships among variables to constructing theory. The model of analysis is inductive. Because of the greater amount of analysis in interpretive case studies, some sources label these case studies "analytical." Analytical case studies are differentiated from straightforward descriptive studies by their complexity, depth, and theoretical orientation (Shaw, 1978).

Evaluative case studies involve description, explanation, and judgment. Much has been written lately about naturalistic evaluation, responsive evaluation, and qualitative evaluation (Guba and Lincoln, 1981; Patton, 1980; Stake, 1981; Goetz and LeCompte, 1984). Guba and Lincoln (1981) review the kinds of reports that might be produced in naturalistic evaluations, and they conclude that case study is the best reporting form. Their rationale recalls the discussion in Chapter One on defining the case study. For them, case study is best because it provides "thick description," is grounded, is holistic and lifelike, simplifies data to be considered by the reader, illuminates meanings, and can communicate tacit knowledge (pp. 375–376). Above all else, though, this type of case study weighs "information to produce judgment. Judging is the final and ultimate act of evaluation" (p. 375).

The case study is a particularly good means of educational evaluation because of its ability to *"explain* the causal links in real-life interventions that are too complex for the survey of experimental strategies. A second application is to *describe* the real-life context in which an intervention has occurred. Third, an evaluation can benefit, again in a generative mode, from an illustrative case study—even a journalistic account—of the intervention itself. Finally, the case study strategy may be used to *explore* those situations in which the intervention being evaluated has no clear, single set of outcomes" (Yin, 1984, p. 25). Case study evaluation of educational issues (or ethnographic evaluations, as they are also called) became "extremely popular in the late 1970's" and have been "the genesis of much educative and basic research since then" (Goetz and LeCompte, 1984, p. 30).

In summary, then, case studies can be identified by their disciplinary orientation, by the end product, or by some combination of the two. Thus in education we have case studies that are ethnographic evaluations, program descriptions, historical interpretations, sociological studies, and so on. While some case studies are purely descriptive, many more are a combination of description and interpretation or description and evaluation.

When to Use a Case Study Design

An investigator may choose among several basic research designs, each of which reveals something different about the phenomenon under study. The question of when to use a qualitative case study for research versus some other design essentially depends upon what the researcher wants to know. How the problem is defined and the questions it raises determine the study's design. Bromley (1986, p. 23) writes that case studies, by definition, "get as close to the subject of interest as they possibly can, partly by means of direct observation in natural settings, partly by their access to subjective factors (thoughts, feelings, and desires), whereas experiments and surveys often use convenient derivative data, e.g. test results, official records. Also, case-studies tend to spread the net for evidence widely, whereas experiments and surveys usually have a narrow focus."

Kenny and Grotelueschen (1980) suggest that several

"preconditions" can help the researcher decide on the appropriateness of using a case study. First, a case study can be considered when "the desired or projected objectives of an educational effort focus on humanistic outcomes or cultural differences, as opposed to behavioral outcomes or individual differences" (p. 3). An example of this situation might be a community literacy program that teaches reading while at the same time empowering adults to take more control of their lives. While quantitative measures might be used to assess "empowerment," data gathered from interviews and perhaps observation would yield more insight into the changes that had occurred.

A case study may also be appropriate when information gleaned from participants is not subject to truth or falsity but "can be subject to scrutiny on the grounds of credibility" (p. 4). In fact, the aim of a case study "is not to find the 'correct' or 'true' interpretation of the facts, but rather to eliminate erroneous conclusions so that one is left with the best possible, the most compelling, interpretation" (Bromley, 1986, p. 38). Suppose, for example, a researcher is interested in employees' opinions on the effectiveness of their company's training program. Of crucial importance here is the individual employee's perspective, not how "true" or "accurate" (by some standard) the account is. A third precondition—one that has already been mentioned as a rationale for a single-case design—is the uniqueness of the situation. Kline's (1981) case study of a back-to-industry program for vocational instructors at a junior college is an example. At the time of her study, only three such programs could be located in the United States.

Paralleling these preconditions, Kenny and Grotelueschen (1980) offer several reasons for choosing a case study design when doing an evaluation: "Case study can be an important approach when the future of a program is contingent upon an evaluation being performed and there are no reasonable indicators of programmatic success which can be formulated in terms of behavioral objectives or individual differences" (p. 5). Case study is appropriate when the objective of an evaluation is "to develop a better understanding of the dynamics of a program. When it is important to be responsive, to convey a holistic and dynamically rich account of an educational program, case study is a tailormade approach" (p. 5). They also argue that a case study design can be justified on the basis that sometimes it is important to leave an account: "This goal of case study is essentially descriptive and of historical significance" (p. 5). Finally, "case study can be supported as the common language approach to evaluation" (p. 5). Using common language, as opposed to scientific or educational jargon, allows the results of a study to be communicated more easily to nonresearchers.

These preconditions are congruent with the four characteristics of case study presented in Chapter One. Case studies are particularistic, descriptive, holistic, and inductive. They also are concerned with understanding and describing process more than behavioral outcomes. Interest in process and interpretation as reasons for using a case study design were pointed out in an early but seminal article on case study (Foreman, 1948, p. 419). Case study, Foreman says, is particularly useful when the problem involves developing a new line of inquiry, needs further conceptualization of factors or functions, "demands emphasis on the *pattern* of interpretation given by subjects," and involves determining "the particular *pattern* of factors significant in a given case."

Process as a focus for case study research can be viewed in two ways: "The first meaning of process is monitoring: describing the context and population of the study, discovering the extent to which the treatment or program has been implemented, providing immediate feedback of a formative type, and the like. The second meaning of process is causal explanation: discovering or confirming the process by which the treatment had the effect that it did" (Reichardt and Cook, 1979, p. 21). Collins and Noblit's (1978) case study of a desegregated high school in Memphis, Tennessee, illustrates the two meanings of process. They discuss the city, the setting, and the extent to which desegregation had been implemented. They also describe how each of the school system's three subsystems (administrative, academic, student) affected the process of interracial schooling. Of particular interest were the differing experiences of the school under two different principals, the climate in the classrooms before and after desegregation, and the students' extracurricular activities. In summarizing the importance of a process rather than an outcome as justification for selecting a case study, Sanders (1981, p. 44) writes: "Case studies help us to understand processes of events, projects, and programs and to discover context characteristics that will shed light on an issue or object."

Strengths and Limitations of Case Study Design

All research designs can be discussed in terms of their relative strengths and limitations. The merits of a particular design are inherently related to the rationale for selecting it as the most appropriate plan for addressing the research problem. One strength of an experimental design, for example, is the predictive nature of the research findings. Because of the tightly controlled conditions, random sampling, and use of statistical probabilities, it is theoretically possible to predict behavior in similar settings without actually observing that behavior. Likewise, if one needs information about the characteristics of a given population or area of interest, a descriptive study is in order. Results, however, would be limited to describing the phenomenon rather than predicting future behavior.

Thus one selects a case study design because of the nature of the research problem and the questions being asked—it is the best plan for answering one's questions. Its strengths outweigh its limitations. The case study offers a means of investigating complex social units consisting of multiple variables of potential importance in understanding the phenomenon. Anchored in real-life situations, the case study results in a rich and holistic account of a phenomenon. It offers insights and illuminates meanings that expand its readers' experiences. These insights can be construed as tentative hypotheses that help structure future research; hence, case study plays an important role in advancing a field's knowledge base. Because of its strengths, case study is a particularly appealing design for applied fields of study such as education. Educational processes, problems, and programs can be examined to bring about understanding that in turn can affect and perhaps even improve practice. Case study has proved particularly useful for studying educational innovations, for evaluating programs, and for informing policy. Collins and Noblit (1978, p. 26) note the strengths of this type of research, which they call field studies, for policy analysis:

> Field research better captures situations and settings which are more amenable to policy and program intervention than are accumulated individual attributes. Second, field studies reveal not static attributes but understanding of humans as they engage in action and interaction within the contexts of situations and settings. Thus inferences concerning human behavior are less abstract than in many quantitative studies, and one can better understand how an intervention may affect behavior in a situation. . . . Field studies are better able to assess social change than more positivistic designs, and change is often what policy is addressing.

The special features of case study research that provide the rationale for its selection also present certain limitations in its usage. Although rich, thick description and analysis of a phenomenon may be desired, one may not have the time or money to devote to such an undertaking. And assuming that one does take the time to produce a worthy case study, the product may be deemed too lengthy, too detailed, or too involved for busy policymakers and educators to read and use. Some suggestions for dealing with reporting and disseminating case studies can be found in the literature, but the amount of description, analysis, or summary material is basically up to the investigator. Guba and Lincoln (1981, p. 377) note an additional limitation of case study narratives: "Case studies can oversimplify or exaggerate a situation, leading the reader to erroneous conclusions about the actual state of affairs." Furthermore, they warn, readers can be seduced into thinking case studies are accounts of the whole: "That is, they tend to masquerade as a whole when in fact they are but a part—a slice of life."

Qualitative case studies are limited, too, by the sensitivity and integrity of the investigator (Riley, 1963). The researcher is

the primary instrument of data collection and analysis. This has
its advantages. But training in observation and interviewing,
though necessary, is not readily available to aspiring case study
researchers. Nor are there guidelines in constructing the final report, and only recently have there been discussions about how
to analyze the data collected. The investigator is left to rely on
his or her own instincts and abilities throughout most of this research effort.

A further concern of case study research—and in particular case study evaluation—is what Guba and Lincoln (1981, p.
378) refer to as "unusual problems of ethics. An unethical case
writer could so select from among available data that virtually
anything he wished could be illustrated." Both the readers of
case studies and the authors themselves need to be aware of
biases that can affect the final product. Clearly related to this
issue of bias is the inherently political nature of case study evaluations. MacDonald and Walker (1977, p. 187) observe that
"educational case studies are usually financed by people who
have, directly or indirectly, power over those studied and por-
trayed." Moreover, "at all levels of the system what people
think they're doing, what they *say* they are doing, what they
appear to others to be doing, and what in fact they *are* doing,
may be sources of considerable discrepancy. . . . Any research
which threatens to reveal these discrepancies threatens to create
dissonance, both personal and political" (p. 186).

Further limitations involve the issues of reliability, validity, and generalizability. There is much debate about how to
interpret these principles. With regard to generalizability, for
example, some assume that one cannot generalize from a case
study and count that as a limitation of the method. Others argue
that rather than applying statistical notions of generalizability
to case studies, one should develop an understanding of generalization that is congruent with the basic philosophy of qualitative inquiry. These issues are discussed more fully in Chapter Ten.

Summary

The disciplines of anthropology, history, psychology, and
sociology have influenced case study research in education. Ter-

minology, theory, and data gathering and analysis techniques from each of these disciplines are used by educators to study problems broadly related to teaching and learning. When the *techniques* of another discipline are employed—for example, participant observation from anthropology or analysis of primary sources from history—the case study is best described as educational. When *concepts* or *theories* are borrowed from another discipline in order to frame the study or interpret the data, the case study is best characterized as being within that discipline's purview. For example, a sociocultural interpretation of some educational practice can be called an ethnographic case study; a historical examination of an educational program can be labeled a historical case study.

Case studies in education also vary in terms of their end product. Some are little more than intensive descriptions of a program, event, or process. Such descriptions are useful in learning about unique or innovative situations and may form a data base for future research. Case studies that go beyond description are interpretive in nature. The researcher uses the data to analyze, interpret, or theorize about the phenomenon. Finally, many case studies are evaluative in that they are undertaken to assess the merit of a particular practice or program. In reality, most case studies are a combination of description and interpretation, or description and evaluation.

The decision to use a case study design is dependent upon the nature of the problem being investigated. The decision is also contingent upon an understanding of the design's inherent strengths and weaknesses. For example, the holistic description is at once a strength and a limitation. Reliance upon the investigator as the primary instrument for data collection and analysis can produce brilliant insights about a phenomenon, or it can produce a pedestrian, incorrect, or even fraudulent analysis. In selecting a research design, something is gained and something is sacrificed. One can only weigh the design's benefits against its limitations and select accordingly.

CHAPTER 3

Defining a Research Problem
and Selecting a Case

Case study research is a legitimate research design in its own right. It should be used when certain questions are raised about a phenomenon and when a certain end product is desired. Case study research is not a substitute for some other design; it has its own special features and functions. Nor should case study be selected by default, as sometimes occurs when a person thinks it will be easier to carry out than some other design. Actually, the opposite may be true. Yin (1984, p. 56), for example, says that the "demands of a case study on a person's intellect, ego, and emotions are far greater than those of any other research strategy."

It is clear that not everyone will feel confident conducting a case study. As with any other design, case study demands certain skills. This chapter begins with a discussion of several characteristics and skills needed to do qualitative case study research. Once a person determines that he or she is suited to doing this type of research, the case must be defined and selected.

Investigator Characteristics

In a *qualitative* case study, the investigator is the primary instrument for gathering and analyzing data. As such, the researcher can respond to the situation by maximizing opportunities for collecting and producing meaningful information. Conversely, the investigator as human instrument is limited by being human—that is, mistakes are made, opportunities are missed, personal biases interfere. Human instruments are as fallible as any other research instrument. The extent to which one has certain personality characteristics and skills necessary for this type of research needs to be assessed, just as one would evaluate a rating scale or survey form in other types of research.

To begin with, the case study researcher must have an enormous *tolerance for ambiguity.* Throughout the case study process, from designing the study, to data collection, to data analysis, there are no set procedures or protocols that one follows step by step. There are guidelines and the experience of others to help, but one must be able to recognize that the "correct" way to proceed will not always be obvious. The very lack of structure is what makes this type of research appealing to many, for it allows the researcher to adapt to unforeseen events and change direction in pursuit of meaning. The investigator's role in qualitative research has often been compared to that of a detective. One must enjoy searching for pieces to the puzzle and tolerate uncertainty for an indefinite period of time. For those who work best in a structured situation and have no patience with ambiguity, a more traditional research design is recommended.

Even designing the study can be stressful to the person who prefers an established format. Decisions have to be made as to just what constitutes the case, how data will be collected, who will be interviewed or observed, what documents will be read, and so on. These procedures are far from routine. Once design decisions are made, gaining access to a site and actually presenting oneself to players in the case can be an unsettling experience. What questions should be asked of whom? What should be observed once on the site? How should the researcher deal with data as they are being collected? And how does that process affect what additional data are needed? At every step of the way, the investigator must exercise discretion. The certainty of predetermined data-analysis procedures is not to be found in this type of research. Case study research thus places the investigator in a largely uncharted ocean. For some it becomes an adventure full of promise for discovery; for others, it can be a disorienting and unproductive experience.

Sensitivity is the second trait demanded by this type of research. The researcher must be sensitive to the context and all the variables within it including the physical setting, the people, the overt and covert agendas, the nonverbal behavior. One also needs to be sensitive to the information being gathered. What does it tell you? How can it direct you to the next piece of data? How well does it reflect what is happening? Finally, one must be aware of one's personal biases and how they may influence the investigation.

This notion of sensitivity pervades the literature on doing qualitative research of any sort. Speaking of evaluators using naturalistic inquiry, Guba and Lincoln (1981, p. 149) make the point that qualitative evaluators do not measure. Rather, "they do what anthropologists, social scientists, connoisseurs, critics, oral historians, novelists, essayists, and poets throughout the years have done. They emphasize, describe, judge, compare, portray, evoke images, and create, for the reader or listener, the sense of having been there."

Being sensitive in the data-gathering phase of a case study involves a keen sense of timing—when to observe more closely, for example, versus knowing when one has observed enough. In interviewing it means knowing when to allow for silence, when to probe more deeply, when to change the direction of the interview. Every sense of the investigator must be alert to cues and nuances provided by the context.

Sensitivity to the data one collects is also important. Most first-time qualitative researchers have trouble "reading" their data. While techniques for analyzing data are being developed and are finding their way into the literature, it is still a highly idiosyncratic, lonely process, the success of which depends on the investigator's sensitivity and analytical powers. In speaking of developing theory from data, Glaser (1978, p. 2) writes:

> At each state of generating theory is reliance on
> the social psychology of the analyst; that is, his

skill, fatigue, maturity, cycling of motivation, life cycle interest, insights into and ideation from the data. Generating theory is done by a human being who is at times intimately involved with and other times quite distant from the data—and who is surely plagued by other conditions in his life. . . . Within the analyst, as the research continues, is a long term biographical and conceptual build up that makes him quite "wise" about the data—how to detail its main problems and processes and how to interpret and explain them theoretically.

To produce a worthwhile case study, the researcher must be sensitive to the biases inherent in this type of research. As Goetz and LeCompte (1984, p. 95) observe, case study research "is one of the few modes of scientific study that admit the subjective perception and biases of both participants and researcher into the research frame." Because the primary instrument in qualitative case study research is human, all observations and analyses are filtered through one's worldview, one's values, one's perspective. It might be recalled that one of the philosophical assumptions underlying this type of research is that reality is not an objective entity; rather, there are multiple interpretations of reality. All research has its biases. But there are ways to deal with investigator bias in qualitative research. "The best cure for biases," write Guba and Lincoln (1981, p. 148), is to be aware of "how they slant and shape what we hear, how they interface with our reproduction of the speaker's reality, and how they transfigure truth into falsity."

Apart from being able to tolerate ambiguity and being a sensitive observer and analyst, a good case study investigator must also be a *good communicator.* A good communicator empathizes with respondents, establishes rapport, asks good questions, and listens intently. Guba and Lincoln (1981, p. 140) write that one of the "hallmarks of outstanding anthropological and sociological studies to date has been the empathy with which they have presented major actors, performers, and informants." Further, they say, "the extent to which inquirers are able to communicate warmth and empathy often marks them as good or not-so-good data collectors."

Empathy is the foundation of rapport. A researcher is better able to have a conversation with a purpose—an interview, in other words—in an atmosphere of trust. "The purpose of interviewing," writes Patton (1980, p. 196), "is to find out what is in and on someone's else's mind." Since what is in and on someone's mind cannot be directly observed or measured, the interviewer has to ask the right question in the right way to obtain meaningful information. Fortunately, interviewing is a skill that can be developed with practice.

Another vital communication skill is being able to listen. The good qualitative researcher "looks and listens everywhere." It is only by listening "to many individuals and to many points of view that value-resonant social contexts can be fully, equitably, and honorably represented" (Guba and Lincoln, 1981, p. 142).

A helpful notion for understanding the importance of communication skills can be found in the anthropological concept of boundary spanning. Boundary spanning is defined as "skill in communicating within and across cultural groups" (Goetz and LeCompte, 1984, p. 99). In its broadest sense,

> boundary spanning involves active participation in a variety of cultures that are involved with and impinge upon a project. . . . An ethnographer needs those skills not only to survive in the research site, but to facilitate execution of the study at every stage. This is because so many constituencies typically develop a vested interest in the project at different times. These may include professional associations, funding agencies, the participants of the study, other academics, and policymaking institutions.
>
> Successful boundary spanning requires familiarity with, or at least the ability to become familiar with, the behaviors, goals, and beliefs of all constituencies that influence a project [Goetz and LeCompte, 1984, p. 100].

There are many lists of the ideal investigator's characteristics in the literature of qualitative research. The three chosen for discussion here—tolerance for ambiguity, sensitivity, and communication skills—capture what most writers consider to be essential for those who conduct this type of research. The question of whether a person can acquire these characteristics, however, has not been answered. If the personality characteristics are present to some degree, they can probably be cultivated; certainly communication skills can be developed to a higher level in almost everyone. Yin (1984) recommends a training session for new researchers. Guba and Lincoln (1981) suggest that people can improve their ability to do this type of research by learning the jargon of the project, by immersing themselves in as many situations as possible in order to gain experience and exposure, and by apprenticing oneself to an experienced qualitative researcher.

The Research Problem

Getting started in case study research involves deciding on the entity to be studied. But one cannot define what the case will be without first having a research problem. Most people understand what it means to have a "problem." A problem in the conventional sense is a matter involving doubt, uncertainty, or difficulty. A person with a problem usually seeks a solution, some clarification, or a decision. So too with a *research* problem. For Dewey (1933, p. 13), a problem is anything that "perplexes and challenges the mind so that it makes belief . . . uncertain." Guba (1978, p. 44) is more specific. For him, a research problem is a "situation resulting from the interaction or juxtaposition of *two or more factors.*" It is this juxtaposition, in Dewey's words, that "perplexes and challenges the mind." There are three basic types of research problem: conceptual, action, and value.

Conceptual problems stem from "two juxtaposed elements that are conceptually or theoretically inconsistent" (Guba, 1978, p. 45). Much of the literature in adult education, for example, states that adults are self-directed and therefore can participate in planning, implementing, and evaluating their own learning. However, studies of adult learners have revealed that some do not know how to take control of their own learning. Since these two notions are theoretically inconsistent, a conceptual problem arises. Is self-direction a precondition of adult learning, or is it one of the goals of an adult learning activity? *Action* problems result from a conflict that seems to provide no clear choice of alternative courses of action. Wanting to know the best method for helping adults learn to read is an example of an action problem. *Value* problems come from "undesirable consequences" according to some standard or other. Allowing prisoners to join an ongoing adult learning class may result in "undesirable consequences" with regard to established patterns of class participation and interaction.

Research problems can arise from a number of sources. McMillan and Schumacher (1984) list personal experience, deductions from theory, related literature, current social and political issues, and practical situations as common sources of research problems. Out of personal experience can come research questions "suggested by observations of certain relationships for which no satisfactory explanation exists, routine ways of doing things that are based on authority or tradition lacking research evidence, or innovations and technological changes that need long-term confirmation" (p. 49). For example, a teacher might observe that all her efforts to include certain students in classroom discussion have failed. Any number of research questions might be asked in this situation. Is there something about these students that they fail to participate? Is it the methods the teacher uses to include them? Is there something about the classroom atmosphere? The personality of the instructor?

Although they are not commonly used in qualitative studies, deductions from theory can lead to good research problems. A case study could be designed, for example, based on the following deduction from theory. In studying male psychosocial development, Levinson (1978) discovered that having a mentor was a crucial factor in men's realizing their young adulthood dream and being successful at midlife. The mentor was approximately eight to fifteen years older, the relationship usually lasted from two to three years, and it was eventually necessary for the protégé to end the relationship in order to be his own man. A case study of a successful midlife man might be undertaken to test Levinson's theory of mentoring.

Problems can be found in related literature and current social and political issues. Nearly every research study has a section with suggestions for future research, many of which could be approached with a qualitative case study design. Issues in society can often be construed as research problems appropriate for educators to investigate. For example: "The women's movement raised questions about sex equity in general and in sex stereotyping of educational materials and practices. The civil rights movement led to research on the education of minority children and the effects of desegregation on racial attitudes, race relations, self-concept, achievement, and the like" (McMillan and Schumacher, 1984, p. 49).

Practical situations, like personal experience, often present research problems especially amenable to evaluation research. "Questions for such research may focus on educational needs; information for program planning, development, and implementation; or the effectiveness of a practice" (p. 49). Which is the best method for teaching math concepts to adults? How can an innovation be implemented in the public school system? What level of funding is needed for vocational programs in the community colleges to prepare young people for jobs?

In identifying a research problem, one moves from general interest, curiosity, or doubt about a situation to a specific statement of the research problem. Translating one's general curiosity into a research problem paves the way for defining the case to be investigated. Most often research problems conducive to a case study design emanate from the everyday world. The researcher

> usually begins with some knowledge of the setting (time, place, participants) and a general idea of the event, such as the introduction of a new program or everyday, common, and recurring events in education. In other words, empirical problems lie all around in varying forms and for the most part need

only to be recognized for their possibilities. There
is almost an intuitive feel for the problem in the
form of such questions as, "I wonder what will
happen now that . . . ," "What does this event really mean to participants?" or "How are they going
to manage to do that?" [McMillan and Schumacher,
1984, p. 310].

Qualitative case study research usually begins with a
problem identified from practice. Then broad questions are
raised. Questions about process (why or how something happens) commonly guide case study research, as do questions of
understanding (what happened, why, and how?). Driessen and
Pyfer (1975), for example, were interested in the difference
that setting might make in adult basic education. Their questions related to understanding the interaction of an informal
setting (the home) with a formal occasion (instruction). In another study (Hardin, 1985), the researcher was interested in
what qualities constitute generativity in midlife, as well as the
process one goes through in becoming generative.

Defining "The Case"

Once the general problem has been identified, the unit of
analysis can be defined. At this point it is assumed that the nature of the questions dictates a qualitative case study design.
What makes the inquiry a case study is "the decision to focus
on enquiry around an instance" (Adelman, Jenkins, and Kemmis, 1983, p. 2). The unit of analysis, or "the case," can be an
individual, a program, an institution, a group, an event, a concept. The key issue in determining the unit of analysis is to decide "what it is you want to be able to say something about at
the end of the study" (Patton, 1980, p. 100).

Consider the following example of how one defines the
unit of analysis using Patton's guideline. One of the most perplexing problems in adult basic education classes is the high attrition rate. Most programs anticipate that upward of half the
students who begin a program will drop out before completion.

Several questions related to this problem would be appropriate for a case study investigation. Does the researcher want to be able to say something about an individual's experience in dropping out of the program? The unit of analysis would be an individual selected for an intensive case investigation. Perhaps of more interest are certain program variables that may affect attrition. The unit of analysis might be a specific instructional technique, teacher style, or location. The researcher might also want to look at the total program. Thus the case study could be a holistic, intensive, rich description and analysis of an individual student's experience, a computer-based instructional program, or the whole program itself. Each of these units constitutes a *bounded system* or "an instance drawn from a class" (here a "class" refers to the attrition problem in adult basic education) (Adelman, Jenkins, and Kemmis, 1983, p. 3).

Determining the unit of analysis for a case study is also influenced by one's philosophical, theoretical, or disciplinary orientation. Sociologists are interested in roles, dyads, subsystems, or total social systems. Psychologists focus on the individual. Political theorists are interested in decision making, programs, implementation processes, and organizational change (Yin, 1984). Educators define their unit of analysis to reflect some aspect of the educational enterprise.

Defining the unit of analysis can be visualized in terms of what Guba and Lincoln (1981) term "bounding problems." Smith (1978), in fact, defines the case as a "bounded system." Bounding problems, according to Guba and Lincoln (p. 86),

> relate to the task of establishing the boundaries of an inquiry as a whole. In experimental inquiry, these boundaries are sharply constrained (controlled), so that there is no question what variables are to be studied, what questions are to be asked, or what hypotheses are to be tested. But in the case of naturalistic inquiry, antecedent conditions are not constrained in any way. Thus the boundary problem comes down to this: How is the inquirer to set limits to his inquiry? What are the rules for

inclusion and exclusion? How can the inquirer
know what is relevant and what is not relevant?

It is the nature of the problem to be investigated that "provides
a major means for setting boundaries" (Guba and Lincoln, 1981,
p. 89).

Adelman, Jenkins, and Kemmis (1983) suggest two ways
that a case or bounded system might be selected for study. First,
an issue is decided upon "and a bounded system (the case) is
selected as an *instance drawn from a class.* For example, a group
of researchers wishing to explore what happens in fringe reli-
gious groups prophesying the end of the world on a stated date
when their prophetic utterances are disconfirmed will select
any instance of such a group" (p. 3). Second, one can be presented with a bounded system "within which issues are indicated, discovered or studied so that a tolerably full understanding of the case is possible. The most straightforward examples
of 'bounded systems' are those in which the boundaries have a
common sense obviousness, e.g. an individual teacher, a single
school, or perhaps an innovatory programme" (p. 3).

The focus of research in a case study is on *one* unit of
analysis. There may be numerous events, participants, or phases
of a process subsumed under the unit. As McMillan and Schumacher (1984, p. 322) observe: "The one unit may be an institution, a program, a process, or an organizational position. A
study may be of one classroom with thirty students or a state
plan to implement a new testing program in three hundred classrooms. The single classroom or the single plan is the unit of
analysis." Eckstein (1975) gives another example of how the
single unit of analysis may contain a diverse number of instances
depending on the focus of the study. If general elections are to
be investigated, for example, the researcher could define the
case in terms of the election system itself ($n = 1$), the six election sites ($n = 6$), or the voters ($n = 120,000,000$).

That the case study focuses on a single unit within which
there may be several examples, events, or situations can be
exemplified by numerous case studies. Offerman (1985) defined
his unit of analysis as consortia of higher education that had

failed. He interviewed personnel and read documents relating to three such consortia. And in a case study of one college's back-to-industry program, Kline (1981) interviewed several dozen participants, observed parts of the program in operation during her site visit, and read all the related documents. She thus had many components related to the case to investigate within her unit of analysis.

Selecting a Sample Within the Case

Thus the researcher first identifies the case, the bounded system, the unit of analysis, to be investigated. The case can be as varied as a second-grade classroom, a systemwide model science program, an individual teacher, or a patient education clinic at a local hospital. Within every case there probably exist numerous sites that could be visited (as in the model science program), events or activities that could be observed, people who could be interviewed, documents that could be read. The researcher thus needs "to consider where to observe, when to observe, whom to observe and what to observe. In short, sampling in field research involves the selection of a research site, time, people and events" (Burgess, 1982, p. 76).

There are two basic types of sampling: probability and nonprobability sampling. Both types have been used in case study research, but nonprobability sampling is the method of choice in *qualitative* case studies. Briefly, the difference between the two types is that in probability sampling "one can specify for each element of the population the probability that it will be included in the sample," whereas "in nonprobability sampling there is no way of estimating the probability that each element has of being included in the sample and no assurance that every element has *some* chance of being included" (Chein, 1981, p. 423). Probability sampling (of which simple random sampling is the most familiar example) allows the investigator to generalize results of the study from the sample to the population from which it was drawn.

Since generalization in a statistical sense is not a goal of qualitative research, probabilistic sampling is not necessary or even justifiable in qualitative research. Anthropologists, for example, have long maintained that nonprobability sampling methods "are logical as long as the fieldworker expects mainly to use his data not to answer questions like 'how much' and 'how often' but to solve *qualitative* problems, such as discovering what occurs, the implications of what occurs, and the relationships linking occurrences" (Honigmann, 1982, p. 84). Thus the most appropriate sampling strategy is nonprobabilistic—the most common form of which is called *purposive* (Chein, 1981) or *purposeful* (Patton, 1980). Purposive sampling is based on the assumption that one wants to discover, understand, gain insight; therefore one needs to select a sample from which one can learn the most. Chein explains:

> The situation is analogous to one in which a number of expert consultants are called in on a difficult medical case. These consultants—also a purposive sample—are not called in to get an average opinion that would correspond to the average opinion of the entire medical profession. They are called in precisely because of their special experience and competence. Or the situation may be viewed as analogous to our more or less haphazard sampling of foods from a famous cuisine. We are sampling, not to estimate some population value, but to get some idea of the variety of elements available in this population [Chein, 1981, p. 440].

Purposive sampling is the same as what Goetz and LeCompte (1984) call *criterion-based sampling.* Criterion-based sampling requires that one establish the criteria, bases, or standards necessary for units to be included in the investigation; one then finds a sample that matches these criteria. The researcher creates a "recipe of the attributes essential to one selected unit and proceed[s] to find or locate a unit that matches the recipe" (Goetz and LeCompte, 1984, p. 77). In Offerman's case study (1985) of failed consortia of higher education, for example, sev-

eral criteria were used to select the sample within the case. To
be included, the failed consortia had to have been in operation
for at least five years, had to have served adult as well as traditional college-age students, and had to have had financial support from sources other than short-term grants.

Both Patton (1980) and Goetz and LeCompte (1984)
enumerate several types of purposeful or criterion-based sampling. These are listed in Table 3.

Table 3. Nonprobability Sampling Strategies.

Purposeful Sampling *(Patton, 1980)*	*Criterion-Based Sampling* *(Goetz and LeCompte, 1984)*

1. Extreme or deviant
2. Typical
3. Maximum variation
4. Critical
5. Politically important or sensitive
6. Convenience
	1. Initial group
	  • comprehensive
	  • quota
	  • network
	  • extreme
	  • typical
	  • unique
	  • reputational
	  • ideal
	  • comparable
	2. Sequential
	  • theoretical
	  • negative
	  • discrepancy

Goetz and LeCompte's schema is somewhat more inclu-
sive than Patton's. Criterion-based sampling strategies can be
used to identify a sample prior to a study or in the early stages.
Using a basic population of high school graduates, an example
of each "initial group" sampling strategy follows:

    Comprehensive: This strategy allows one to "examine
    every case, instance, or element in a relevant popula-
    tion" (p. 78). Example: All graduates of a particular
    high school.
    Quota selection: Researchers "identify the major, rele-
    vant subgroups of some given universe" and "then pro-

ceed to obtain some arbitrary number of participants in each category" (p. 79). Example: Five graduates from each of the last ten classes.

Network selection: "Each successive participant or group is named by a preceding group or individual." The sample is collected on the basis of participant referrals (p. 79). Example: Graduates name other graduates who have remained in the area since graduation.

Extreme-case selection: After the norm for a typical case is established, researchers "seek instances reflecting the extremes, or poles . . . so that comparisons against the norms may be made" (p. 81). Example: Graduates who later received doctorates or who became convicted criminals.

Typical-case selection: "The researcher develops a profile of attributes possessed by an average case and then seeks an instance of this case" (p. 81). Example: Any who meet the criteria of a typical graduate of the particular school.

Unique-case selection: Selection is based on "unique or rare attributes inherent in a population" such as an "exceptional innovative program" or unusual ethnic composition (p. 82). Example: A graduate who becomes a professional athlete.

Reputational-case selection: Instances are chosen "on the recommendation of experienced experts in an area" (p. 82). Example: The principal chooses students based on a researcher's requirements for the sample.

Ideal-typical-bellwether-case selection: "The researcher develops a profile of an instance that would be the best, most efficient, most effective, or most desirable of some population and then finds a real-world case that most closely matches the profile" (p. 82). Example: Any graduate who meets the criteria of an "ideal" graduate.

Comparable-case selection: Selecting individuals, groups, sites, and so forth on the same relevant characteristics over a period of time in order to compare results. It is "the ethnographer's version of replication" (p. 83). Example: Selecting the same type of graduate from several graduating classes.

Some qualitative research designs incorporate an ongoing sample selection process. Goetz and LeCompte (1984) call this "sequential" criterion-based sampling, which includes theoretical sampling and negative-case and discrepant-case selection. *Theoretical sampling* has been popularized by Glaser and Strauss (1967) in their book *The Discovery of Grounded Theory:* "Theoretical sampling is the process of data collection for generating theory whereby the analyst jointly collects, codes, and analyzes his data and decides what data to collect next and where to find them, in order to develop his theory as it emerges" (p. 45). The data lead the investigator to the next document to be read, the next person to be interviewed, and so on. The researcher asks: "For what theoretical purpose are the groups and subgroups used? Theoretical sampling, therefore, forces researchers to consider what groups to observe, when to observe them, when to stop observing them, and what data to gather" (Burgess, 1982, p. 75). It is an evolving process guided by the emerging theory—hence "theoretical" sampling. Analysis occurs simultaneously as one identifies the sample and collects the data. "The analyst who uses theoretical sampling cannot know in advance precisely what to sample for and where it will lead him. . . . It is never clear cut for what and to where discovery will lead. It is ongoing" (Glaser, 1978, p. 37). As data are being collected and theoretical constructs begin to evolve, one might also look for exceptions (negative-case selection) or variants (discrepant-case selection) to emerging findings. These are other forms of sequential sampling mentioned by Goetz and LeCompte (1984).

Thus the questions, concerns, and philosophical assumptions characteristic of qualitative case studies lead to forms of nonprobability sampling in determining the sample of instances, locations, people, times, and so on to be included in the case. Purposive and criterion-based sampling occur before the data are gathered, whereas theoretical sampling is done in conjunction with data collection.

Summary

It is clear that not everyone would feel at ease with a case study design. The researcher is the primary instrument for data collection and analysis and as such must possess certain characteristics in order to produce a good case study. The investigator must have an enormous tolerance for ambiguity, must be a good communicator, and must be highly sensitive to the context, to the data, and to personal bias. While several of these skills can be developed, the researcher should feel some initial confidence in his or her predisposition to this type of research.

Selecting the case to be investigated involves understanding that the case is a single unit or a bounded system within which there may be numerous situations, participants, events, or phases of a process. Since it is impossible to interview *everyone*, observe *everything*, and gather *all* the relevant materials in a case, a sample needs to be selected either before data collection begins or while the data are being gathered. The most appropriate sampling strategy for a qualitative case study is nonprobability sampling, of which there are several forms. Purposive and theoretical sampling are well-known and widely used sampling strategies in qualitative research.

CHAPTER 4

Handling Theory
and Literature Reviews
in Case Study Research

There are at least two senses in which the idea of theory is important in research. The first is how an investigator's theoretical orientation to research shapes the research process. Approached from another perspective is the matter of theory's relationship to the study's content or topic. Some case study research tests theory whereas *qualitative* case studies build theory. This chapter explains how one's theoretical orientation affects research activity and how theory functions in case study research. The chapter also deals with how to take account of previous studies and literature pertinent to the research topic.

The Investigator's Worldview

How the investigator views the world affects the entire research process—from conceptualizing a problem, to collecting and analyzing data, to interpreting the findings. A theoretical perspective "is a way of looking at the world, like assumptions people have about what is important, and what makes the world work" (Bogdan and Biklen, 1982, p. 30).

Even before an investigation begins, theoretical orientation plays a role, for the researcher has been socialized into a
discipline that has its own vocabulary, concepts, and theories
(Goetz and LeCompte, 1984). One begins to think like a member of the discipline and to view the world through the discipline's lens. This perspective affects the nature of the questions
raised, which in turn determines the research design, which in
turn influences the conclusions drawn. An educator, a sociologist, and a political scientist could all look at the same phenomenon, say a school, and, viewing the school through the
lenses of the different disciplines, see different problems and
raise very different questions. All three research investigations
would thus differ in terms of:

1. The focus and purpose of the study and the
    questions it addresses;
2. The research model or design used and justifi-
    cation for its choice;
3. The participants or subjects of the study and
    the setting(s) and context(s) investigated;
4. Researcher experience and roles assumed in
    the study;
5. Data collection strategies used in the study;
6. Techniques used to analyze the data collected
    during the study; and
7. Findings of the study and their interpretations
    and applications [Goetz and LeCompte, 1984,
    pp. 34–35].

These seven stages represent decision points in the research process. Each point—from which question to address to which
interpretation to advance—is a function of the researcher's theoretical orientation.

A theoretical orientation is analogous to, perhaps synonymous with, how some authorities define paradigm. Bogdan and
Biklen (1982, p. 30) define paradigm as "a loose collection of
logically held-together assumptions, concepts, or propositions
that orient thinking and research." For Lincoln and Guba (1985,

p. 15), a paradigm is "a systematic set of beliefs, together with their accompanying methods. . . . Paradigms represent a distillation of what we *think* about the world (but cannot prove)." They describe three major paradigms in the history of social science inquiry—prepositivist, positivist, and postpositivist, of which naturalistic inquiry is a form.

The assumptions of the naturalistic paradigm (or qualitative research, as it is termed in this book) orient thinking about research just as one's disciplinary training influences the research process in the manner outlined above. Thus if the researcher's theoretical orientation is naturalistic or qualitative, his or her research would be characterized by the following: natural settings, humans as primary data-gathering instruments, use of tacit knowledge, qualitative methods, purposive sampling, inductive data analysis, grounded theory, emergent design, negotiated outcomes, case-study reporting mode, idiographic interpretation, tentative application of findings, focus-determined boundaries, and special criteria for trustworthiness (Lincoln and Guba, 1985, pp. 39–43).

Types of Theory

The role of theory in research can be thought of in terms of an investigator's theoretical orientation, or it can be approached in terms of how theory relates to the problem under investigation. Since "theory" is defined in numerous ways and there are different types of theory, one writer has concluded that "a theory is what a given author says it is" (Knowles, 1984, p. 5). Nevertheless, a theory integrates pieces of information into a whole; it makes sense out of data; it summarizes what is known and offers a general explanation of the phenomenon under study. Theories may be regarded as deductive models or pattern models. Kerlinger's (1986, p. 9) often quoted definition of theory as a "set of interrelated constructs (concepts), definitions, and propositions that present a systematic view of phenomena by specifying relations among variables, with the purpose of explaining and predicting the phenomena" would be, in Kaplan's (1964) analysis, a deductive definition of theory. It is deductive as opposed to a pattern model because it involves general laws, deduction of unknowns from knowns, and prediction.

Pattern theories, on the other hand, are better suited to qualitative inquiry (Lincoln and Guba, 1985) because "something is explained when it is so related to a set of other elements that together they constitute a unified system. We understand something by identifying it as a specific part in an organized whole" (Kaplan, 1964, p. 333). Prediction entails deduction in contrast to the inclusiveness of a pattern theory that "can be indefinitely filled in and extended: as we obtain more and more knowledge it continues to fall into place in this pattern, and the pattern itself has a place in a larger whole" (p. 335). Kaplan further explains the difference between a deductive and a pattern model: "Rather than saying that we understand something when we have an explanation for it, the pattern model says that we have an explanation for something when we understand it" (p. 335). A pattern theory is analogous to Glaser and Strauss's (1967) concept of grounded theory, which will be discussed in more detail shortly.

The level of explanation and the range of phenomena to which a theory refers determine what type of theory it is. Again definitions vary, but it is helpful to note the general differences, at least, among grand, middle-range, and substantive theory.

Grand theory attempts to explain large categories of phenomena and is most common in the natural sciences. Newton, Einstein, Darwin, and Mendel have constructed grand theories as have Toynbee and Parsons in the social sciences (Goetz and LeCompte, 1984). However, some believe human behavior to be too complex for us to fashion universal laws in the same manner as laws are discovered in the natural sciences. For the most part, grand theories have had little application in education, nor have theories of this scope been developed through educational research.

Middle-range theory falls between "the minor working hypotheses of everyday life and the all-inclusive grand theories" (Glaser and Strauss, 1967, p. 33). These theories "address one area of human experience, conceptually abstracted, and emphasize an explicit data base as their foundation" (Goetz and

LeCompte, 1984, p. 37). Goetz and LeCompte regard theories of cognition and learning, social learning, and life-span development as middle-range.

Even more specific is *substantive theory*. These theories are restricted to particular settings, groups, times, populations, or problems. In adult education, for example, substantive theory may deal with reentry women, adult basic education programs, or math anxiety. This level of theory is closely related to real-life situations. In Glaser and Strauss's (1967) view, substantive theory is grounded in the empirical world. Substantive theory is particularly prevalent in applied fields such as education. It derives from practice and is in turn suitable for practical situations.

These three levels of theory are not as discrete as they appear to be on paper, nor is there even consensus regarding terminology. Glaser and Strauss (1967), for example, place substantive theory in the middle-range category along with "formal" theory, which is somewhat more abstract than substantive theory. Denzin (1970) distinguishes among grand, middle-range, formal, and substantive theory. Goetz and LeCompte (1984) equate formal with middle-range theory. What is important is that "theory" means different things to different people. Its role in research—and case study research in particular—can be better understood if we recognize how theory is being defined and what type of theory we are referring to.

Theory in Case Study Research

A case study design can be used to test theory, but a *qualitative* case study usually builds theory. Case study is thus tied to theory either "as a receptacle for putting theories to work" or "as a catalytic element in the unfolding of theoretical knowledge" (Eckstein, 1975, p. 100). The place of theory in a case study depends to a large extent upon what is known in the area of interest. In some areas of social science research, a considerable amount of data has already been gathered and interpreted by theory; in other areas less is known and there are fewer theories. Thus, depending on the state of knowledge and amount of theory, a case study might test theory, clarify, refine, or extend theory, or, in qualitative case studies, develop new theory.

Much research in general is guided by prior theory—that is, deductions are made from existing theory about corresponding behavior or events in the real world. These deductions, usually in the form of hypotheses, are tested and, to the extent that they can be verified, the theory becomes more credible. One decides in advance which principles will be applied to interpreting specific phenomena. The theory provides a framework for what is to be observed and what is to be collected in the form of data. Empirical evidence then confirms or refutes the theory. When a theory is being tested, control of extraneous variables is an important consideration; equal concern must also be given to the number and representativeness of the cases used to test the theory.

A case study that tests theory begins with reference to a theory from which deductions are made—that is, an investigator deduces that if the theory is valid then a specific event or action should occur in a particular manner. Piaget's theory of cognitive development, for example, posits that children move through four stages of cognitive growth, reaching the last stage of formal operations sometime in the early teens. If his theory is valid, then adults past the teen years should be at the stage of formal operations. An intensive case study of a single adult could verify the theory, refute the theory if the adult were not at the fourth stage, or possibly extend the theory—if, for example, the adult engaged in formal operations in certain circumstances and not in others.

Understanding and interpreting the findings of a case investigation in light of established theory serves to test theory. Valid theories "*compel* particular case interpretations. The import of that possibility . . . lies in the corollary that a case might invalidate a theory, if an interpretation of the case compelled by the theory does not fit" (Eckstein, 1975, p. 104). Eckstein compares using a crucial case to test theory with an experiment designed to test a law in the physical sciences: If a well-constructed experiment can test theory, "then so may a well-chosen case—one that is somehow crucial for a theory as are certain experiments (or indeed natural observations) in the physical sciences" (p. 117). Besides a "crucial" case, one might also use what Goetz and LeCompte (1984) call "extreme," "unique," "representational," or "typical" cases to test theory.

In education, the case study design is almost never used to test theory (Hammersley, Scarth, and Webb, 1985). Perhaps this says something about the state of theory building in this field or perhaps it is a comment on the status of case study as a research methodology. The qualitative case study has been widely used, however, in the service of constructing theory. It becomes necessary to build theory when there is none available to explain a particular phenomenon or when existing theory does not provide an adequate or appropriate explanation. Eckstein (1975, p. 104) calls theory-building case studies "heuristic" because they aim "to find out."

Case studies that are undertaken to build theory use an inductive rather than deductive mode of thinking about the problem and analyzing the data. These studies, which have as their goal discovery of theory rather than verification, partake of the qualitative or naturalistic paradigm discussed in Chapter One. Because there is little or no theory to aid in designing the study, there is little or no manipulation of variables and no predetermined outcomes. Rather, inductive case studies "permit intensive analysis that does not commit the researcher to a highly limited set of variables and thus increases the probability that critical variables and relations will be found" (Eckstein, 1975, p. 106).

This is not to say that a researcher enters an investigation with a blank mind. As mentioned earlier, every researcher holds assumptions, concepts, or theory. Riley (1963, pp. 5–6) observes that the research process begins with at least an "organizing image of the phenomenon to be investigated" and "the selection of facts and the searching for order among them is guided by some prior notions or theories about the nature of the social phenomenon under study." Even in a comprehensive case study "one cannot exhaust the description of a setting." Therefore, "there must always be selection criteria and these are derived, in part at least, from theoretical assumptions, from ideas about what produces what" (Hammersley, Scarth, and Webb, 1985, p. 54). Patton (1980, p. 277) notes that every researcher has "theoretical predispositions" that affect the focus of a study.

Armed with an interest in a particular phenomenon and perhaps some notions about what one might find, case study investigators immerse themselves in the totality of the case. As the setting becomes familiar, and as data are being collected, the researcher looks for underlying patterns—conceptual categories that make sense out of the phenomenon. Exactly how one "sees" relationships among pieces of data or, in short, "discovers" theory cannot be precisely explained. Theory building comes from the insights of a sensitive observer (Glaser and Strauss, 1967). The insights that form the basis of new theory can come from one's imagination, personal experience, the experiences of others, and existing theory. The trick in using existing theory as a source for new theory "is to line up what one takes as theoretically possible or probable with what one is finding in the field" (Glaser and Strauss, 1967, p. 253). The process is one of flexible interaction between phenomenon and theory.

Although the act of discovery cannot be precisely formulated, there are techniques one can use to uncover patterns in the data. Glaser and Strauss (1967) advocate a method of constant comparative analysis consisting of four stages. In the first stage, incidents are compared and tentative categories and/or properties are generated. In the second stage, the level of comparison changes from "incident with incident" to "incident with properties of the category" (Glaser and Strauss, 1967, p. 108). In the third stage, similar categories are reduced to a small number of highly conceptual categories, hypotheses are proposed, and data are checked for their fit into the overall framework. The fourth stage is the actual writing of the theory from coded data. Guba and Lincoln (1981), Patton (1980), Bogdan and Biklen (1982), and Goetz and LeCompte (1984) also discuss how to handle data inductively. These and other strategies for analyzing case study data are discussed in more depth in Chapter Eight.

In summary, then, theory permeates the entire process of case study research. The very questions an investigator raises derive from the theoretical orientation of his or her discipline. From the initial formulation of the problem through to the interpretation of findings, theory informs the choices one makes. The process is interactive and flexible. Finally, case study designs can be used to test, refine, or extend existing theory—or, more likely, a qualitative case study can be used to discover new theoretical constructs.

Functions of the Literature Review

All research should take into account previous work in the same area. An investigator who ignores prior research and theory chances pursuing a trivial problem, duplicating a study already done, or repeating others' mistakes. The goal of research —contributing to the knowledge base of the field—may then never be realized. "The value of any single study is derived as much from how it fits with and expands on previous work as from the study's intrinsic properties." And if some studies seem more significant than others, it is "because the piece of the puzzle they solve (or the puzzle they introduce) is extremely important, not because they are solutions in and of themselves" (Cooper, 1984, p. 9). This section on the literature review addresses the following questions: What is a literature review? Why do a review? When do you do one? How do you go about it?

A literature review interprets and synthesizes what has been researched and published in the area of interest. The literature itself consists of two types: data-based research studies and non-data-based writings. Data-based research refers to studies that involve the collection and analysis of data gathered from people, organizations, documents, and so on. Non-data-based writings reflect the writer's experiences or opinions and can range from the highly theoretical to popular testimonials. The amount of each type of literature to be found varies with the problem. There are many data-based studies to be reviewed on the topic of participation in adult education, for example. On the other hand, most of the literature on theories of adult learning is conceptual, since few theories have been empirically tested.

A literature review can be independent of any other

work. The thrust of an independent literature review is to present the state of the art with regard to a certain topic. Such reviews usually assess the work to date and may even offer suggestions for future inquiry. The great majority of literature reviews, however, are introductions to new data; they are part of a study; they form part of the foundation for the new study at hand. Depending on the problem, either type of literature review could be characterized as primarily integrative, theoretical, or methodological (Cooper, 1984). *Integrative* reviews summarize past research; *theoretical* reviews focus on relevant theories; *methodological* reviews concentrate on research methods and definitions. In practice, most reviews integrate all relevant information on a topic, whether the information is from previous investigations, theory, or methodology.

Investigators who do not take the time to find out what has already been thought or researched may be missing an opportunity to make a significant contribution to their field. Indeed, one function of the literature review is to provide the foundation for contributing to the knowledge base. No problem in education exists in isolation from other areas of human behavior. Consequently, there is always some research study, some theory, some thinking related to the problem that can be reviewed to inform the study at hand.

Besides providing a foundation for the problem to be investigated, the literature review can demonstrate how the present study "advances, refines, or revises what is already known" (Merriam and Simpson, 1984, p. 30). It is important to know how your study deviates from what has already been done. Conversely, a researcher who wants to replicate a study must defend the need for replication by assessing the "methodological strengths and deficiencies present in earlier, significant studies" (Merriam and Simpson, 1984, p. 30).

A literature review can do more than set the stage for a study, however. The process can contribute to formulating the problem and answering specific design questions. Knowing what hypotheses have been advanced and tested previously, how terms have been defined, and what assumptions have been dealt with by other investigators can simplify the researcher's task. And knowing what research designs have been used before, and with what success, can save an investigator from wasting time and money. Finally, "a review of the literature may uncover survey instruments, tests, and other measures that have already been validated and thus save the researcher the trouble of designing a valid and reliable instrument" (Merriam and Simpson, 1984, pp. 30-31).

The literature review can help in the formulation of the problem, in the selection of methodology, and in the interpretation of research results. The findings of a study are best interpreted in light of what was previously known about the topic. Linking specific findings to previous work demonstrates to the reader just how this study contributes to the developing knowledge base of the field. And the study's contribution, of course, determines its significance.

There is little doubt that a literature review can strengthen a research study in several ways. Determining the best time to conduct the review, however, is a matter of some debate. Most writers would agree that the task of becoming familiar with the background of a topic is best undertaken early in the research process. A literature review's impact on problem formulation is an interactive process. At one end of a continuum is reviewing the literature to *find* a problem; at the other end is reviewing the literature to see if the investigator's problem has ever been studied. Somewhere in the middle we find the investigator who has some notion about what he or she wants to research and consults the literature for help in focusing the problem.

As discussed in Chapter One, how one defines the problem may determine whether one proceeds inductively or deductively. That is, the study may be exploratory, and develop theory, or it may be hypothetical-deductive and test theory. Case study designs can be used in the service of either mode of inquiry. While a literature review helps in problem formulation regardless of design, its prominence in inductive research may be considerably less than in theory-testing studies. Glaser (1978, p. 31) addresses this difference:

> In deductive research the analyst first reads the literature of the field to the fullest coverage possible, from which he deducts or synthesizes a framework,

usually theoretical, to study and verify in his research. . . . He then collects the data according to
the concepts of the framework. . . . Because of his
initial scholarship and deduction his findings are directly woven into the literature of the field. . . .

In our approach we collect the data in the
field first. Then start analyzing it and generating theory. When the theory seems sufficiently grounded
and developed, *then* we review the literature in the
field and relate the theory to it through the integration of ideas. . . . Thus scholarship in the same
area starts after the emerging theory is sufficiently
developed so the theory will not be preconceived
by preempting concepts.

Glaser is clear that even in inductive, grounded theory studies,
it is essential to read widely. He suggests reading in substantive
areas somewhat different from the research area at first, then
reading in one's own area as the research gets under way. The
activity is then highly relevant, for the researcher can "skip and
dip, thereby gaining greater coverage, since he now has a clear
purpose for covering his field, which is to integrate his generated theory with the other literature in the field" (Glaser, 1978,
p. 32). In the qualitative case study, one "should read for ideas,
whether the ideas are in the work or in generating his own ideas.
. . . Ideas, of course, make one theoretically sensitive, and the
more ideas and the more they connect tend to make the analyst
sensitive to what he may discover in his data" (p. 32).

Conducting a Literature Review

How does one actually conduct a literature review? This
topic is covered in more depth in other sources than we can go
into here (Cooper, 1984; McMillan and Schumacher, 1984; Merriam and Simpson, 1984). Nevertheless, the reader might find
helpful a summary of the steps involved. First, search for literature that might be selected for review. The scope of the search
is determined by how well defined the research problem is, as

well as one's prior familiarity with the topic. Those with only a vague sense of the problem might start with an overview of the topic that can be gotten from subject encyclopedias, handbooks, and yearbooks. Major studies, theories, issues, and so on can be identified in this way. The next step is to check bibliographies, indexes, and abstracts that reference specific aspects of a topic. This step in the search is typically done by computer. Computer searches can access data bases with speed and breadth of coverage not possible by hand.

Once a set of references and abstracts has been collected, the researcher must decide which full-length resources should be obtained and then which resources to include in the review. This selection can be made on the basis of the following criteria:

- Is the author of the source an authority on the topic—one who has done much of the empirical work in the area or one who has offered seminal theory upon which subsequent research and writing has been based? If so, that author's work will be quoted by others and listed in bibliographies on the topic.
- When was the article or book or report written? As a rule, the most recent work in an area should be included in a review.
- What exactly was written about or tested? If a particular resource or research study is highly relevant to your present research interest, it should be included even if the "who" and "when" criteria are not met.
- What is the quality of the source? A thoughtful analysis, a well-designed study, or an original way of viewing the topic is probably a significant piece of literature [Merriam and Simpson, 1984, pp. 36–37].

Knowing when to stop reviewing the literature is as important as knowing where and how to locate sources. A sense of being saturated signals the end of the search. When you begin encountering familiar references and have stopped finding significant new resources, it is time to quit.

The next step in the process is to evaluate each piece of

literature selected for review. Depending on the nature of the literature, any number of criteria can be used to assess its worth and contribution to the field. In any case, a critical review of the literature demands more than listing or describing what has been written or researched. The end product is "a narrative essay that integrates, synthesizes, and critiques the important thinking and research on a particular topic" (Merriam and Simpson, 1984, p. 38). The structure of the final written review emerges from the nature of the particular literature reviewed. A review of the literature on learning styles, for example, might contain sections on conceptualizations of learning style, instruments that measure learning style, populations that have been used in learning style research, and so on.

Summary

Conducting a literature review is a vital component of the research process. Familiarity with previous research and theory in the area of study can help in conceptualizing the problem, conducting the study, and interpreting the findings. The question of *when* to review the literature depends on whether the case study is selected to test theory or to build theory. The question of *where* to place a review of previous work in a case study report is discussed in Chapter Eleven.

Although the role of theory and the role of the literature review were covered as separate topics in this chapter, they are in fact activities that are closely related in conducting case study research. It is from a review of the literature that one discovers what theory exists on a topic and how well the theory has been verified through testing. Previous research and theory in an area can offer helpful guidance in the design of a new study. A review also assures the investigator that the study has not already been done.

Furthermore, theory and previous research help delineate the problem to be studied. Likewise, one is guided to a specific body of literature by the emerging problem. Knowledge of previous work and theory also affects the choice of data collection methods, a topic discussed in the next three chapters.

PART TWO

MASTERING QUALITATIVE DATA COLLECTION METHODS

Data are nothing more than ordinary bits and pieces of information found in the environment. They can be concrete and measurable, as in class attendance, or invisible and difficult to measure, as in feelings. Whether or not a bit of information becomes data in a research study depends solely on the interest and perspective of the investigator. The way in which rainwater drains from the land may be "data" to a soil scientist, for example, but not even noticed by the homeowner. Likewise activity patterns in a school cafeteria, while holding no interest to students, staff, or faculty, may be of great interest to someone studying students' behavior outside the classroom.

Data conveyed through words have been labeled "qualitative," whereas data presented in number form are "quantitative." Case studies of the type discussed in this book make extensive use of qualitative data. Qualitative data consist of *detailed descriptions* of situations, events, people, interactions, and observed behaviors; *direct quotations* from people about

their experiences, attitudes, beliefs, and thoughts; and excerpts
or entire passages from documents, correspondence, records,
and case histories" (Patton, 1980, p. 22). These descriptions,
quotations, and excerpts are "raw data from the empirical
world, . . . data which provide *depth* and *detail*" (p. 22).

The depth and detail of qualitative data can be obtained
only by "getting close," physically and psychologically, "to the
phenomenon under study" (Patton, 1980, p. 43). As Lofland
writes: "The commitment to get close, to be factual, descriptive and quotive, constitutes a significant commitment to represent the participants *in their own terms. . . .* A major methodological consequence of these commitments is that the qualitative
study of people *in situ* is a *process of discovery.* It is of neces-
sity a process of learning what is happening. . . . It is the observer's task to find out what is fundamental or central to the
people or world under observation" (Lofland, quoted in Patton, 1980, pp. 36–37).

In contrast to qualitative data conveyed through words or
images, quantitative data is presented in numerical form. It is
the quantification of a quality—that is, rather than describing
the nature of a belief, attitude, event, or behavior, emphasis is
placed on measuring the extent to which it exists. Quantitative
data can tell us how many, how much, and how it is distributed.

There is a sense, however, in which all data are inherently qualitative. That is, before something can be quantified, it
has to be identified, named, described, understood. "Behind
any number on a computer printout, and descriptive equation,
or any punch on an IBM card lies a qualitative source" (Ratcliffe, 1983, p. 149). Furthermore, both qualitative and quantitative data are interpretations of experience. In one case the
experience is mediated through words; in the other situation,
through numbers. "Numbers, equations, and words share similar
properties: they are all abstract, symbolic representations of
reality, but they are not reality itself" (Ratcliffe, 1983, p. 150).

Qualitative case studies rely heavily upon qualitative data
obtained from interviews, observations, and documents. Quantitative data from surveys or other instruments can be used to
support findings from qualitative data. Sieber (1982) details
four ways in which data from quantitative surveys can help in

the understanding of field observations. First, these data can correct what he calls the "holistic fallacy"—that is, they can help the researcher guard against assuming that all aspects of a situation fit an emerging theory. Second, quantitative data can be used in support of a generalization made from a single or limited observation. Third, observations based on fieldwork can be verified. And fourth, "survey results can cast a new light on field observations, or more precisely, the serendipitous nature of some survey findings can illuminate a field observation that was hitherto inexplicable or misinterpreted" (p. 187).

The use of multiple methods of collecting data is one form of what Denzin (1970, p. 301) calls *triangulation* (see also Mathison, 1988). Methodological triangulation combines dissimilar methods such as interviews, observations, and physical evidence to study the same unit. "The rationale for this strategy is that the flaws of one method are often the strengths of another, and by combining methods, observers can achieve the best of each, while overcoming their unique deficiencies" (Denzin, 1970, p. 308). The opportunity to use multiple methods of data collection is a major strength of case study research exceeding "that in other research strategies, such as experiments, surveys, or histories. Experiments, for instance, are largely limited to the measurement and recording of actual behavior and generally do not include the systematic use of survey or verbal information. Surveys tend to be the opposite, emphasizing verbal information but not the measurement or recording of actual behavior. Finally, histories are limited to events in the 'dead' past and therefore seldom have any contemporary sources of evidence, such as direct observations of a phenomenon or interviews with key actors" (Yin, 1984, p. 90).

Part Two of this book focuses on the data collection techniques most appropriate for qualitative case study research. The three chapters in Part Two thus explore how to collect and record data from interviews of persons involved in or knowledgeable about the phenomenon under study, from observations of people, activities, programs, or events, and from documents. *Documents* is a term used broadly in this book to refer to printed and other materials relevant to the case, including archival records, personal papers, photographs, and physical artifacts.

CHAPTER 5

Conducting
Effective Interviews

Throughout the process of doing a case study, investigators continually make decisions, choose among alternatives, and exercise judgment. Once the research problem has been identified, the unit of analysis—the case—must be selected. Next the investigator must decide what information will be needed to address the problem and how best to obtain that information. Interviewing is a common means of collecting qualitative data. Discussed in this chapter are types of interviews, the nature of the interaction between interviewer and respondent, beginning the interview, asking good questions, and recording and evaluating interview data.

Interview Data

In case study research of contemporary education, some and occasionally all of the data are collected through interviews. The most common form of interview is the person-to-person encounter in which one person elicits information from another. Group or panel formats can also be used to obtain data. In any case, an interview is a conversation—but a "conversation with a purpose" (Webb and Webb quoted in Burgess, 1982, p. 107). In qualitative case study research, the main purpose of an interview is to obtain a special kind of information. The researcher wants to find out what is "in and on someone else's mind." Patton (1980) explains further: "We interview people to find out from them those things we cannot directly observe. . . . We cannot observe feelings, thoughts, and intentions. We cannot observe behaviors that took place at some previous point in time. We cannot observe situations that preclude the presence of an observer. We cannot observe how people have organized the world and the meanings they attach to what goes on in the world—we have to ask people questions about those things. The purpose of interviewing, then, is to allow us to enter into the other person's perspective" (p. 196).

Interviewing is necessary when we cannot observe behavior, feelings, or how people interpret the world around them. It is also necessary to interview when we are interested in past events that are impossible to replicate. For example, school psychologists might be interested in the reaction of students who witnessed a teacher being attacked at school. Likewise, a catastrophic event such as a nuclear accident or natural disaster cannot be replicated, but its effects on a community might be the focus of a case study investigation. Interviewing is also the best technique to use when conducting intensive case studies of individuals as Robert Coles did in *Children of Crisis* (1967). Conversely, interviewing is selected when one wants to study "a relatively large number of people in a relatively short period of time" in order to obtain "a broad picture of a range of settings, situations, or people" (Taylor and Bogdan, 1984, p. 79). Lillian Rubin's study (1985) of friendship in which she interviewed three hundred men and women from diverse backgrounds is such an example. In short, the decision to use interviewing as one's primary mode of data collection should be based on the kind of information needed and whether interviewing is the best way to get it. Dexter (1970, p. 11) summarizes when to use interviewing: "Interviewing is the preferred tactic of data collection when . . . it will get *better* data or *more* data or data *at less cost* than other tactics!"

Types of Interviews

The most common way of deciding which type of interview to use is by determining the amount of structure desired. On a continuum, highly structured questionnaire-driven interviews would be at one pole and open-ended, conversational formats at the other. In highly structured interviews, questions and the order in which they are asked are determined ahead of time. The most structured interview is actually an oral form of the written survey. The U.S. Census Bureau and marketing surveys are good examples of what Denzin (1970, p. 123) calls the "schedule standardized interview." This type of structured interview is used when a large sample is to be surveyed, when hypotheses are to be tested, or when quantification of results is important. Four assumptions underlie the schedule standardized interview:

1.   The respondents have a common vocabulary.
2.   Questions can be devised that are equally meaningful to every respondent.
3.   Not only do the questions have a common meaning, but so does the context in which they are asked, including the interview context itself.
4.   The preceding three assumptions can be met through a pilot investigation (Denzin, 1970, pp. 123–124).

As noted, this type of interviewing is a form of traditional survey research. Interviewing for case study research, especially *qualitative* case studies, may use this highly structured format to gather common sociodemographic data from respondents. For the most part, however, interviewing is more open-ended and less structured. Less structured formats assume that individual respondents define the world in unique ways. The purpose of the interview, then, is "*not* to put things in someone else's mind (for example, the interviewer's perceived categories for organizing the world) but rather to access the perspective of the person being interviewed" (Patton, 1980, p. 196).

Less structured alternatives to the schedule standardized interview are available to the qualitative case study researcher.

In the semistructured interview, certain information is desired from all the respondents. These interviews are guided by a list of questions or issues to be explored, but neither the exact wording nor the order of the questions is determined ahead of time. This format allows the researcher to respond to the situation at hand, to the emerging worldview of the respondent, and to new ideas on the topic.

Unstructured interviews are particularly useful when the researcher does not know enough about a phenomenon to ask relevant questions. Thus there is no predetermined set of questions and the interview is essentially exploratory. One of the goals of the unstructured interview is, in fact, learning enough about a situation to formulate questions for subsequent interviews. Thus the unstructured interview is often used in conjunction with participant observation in the early stages of a case study. It takes a skilled researcher to handle the great flexibility demanded by the unstructured interview. Insights and understanding can be obtained in this approach, but at the same time an interviewer may feel lost in a sea of divergent viewpoints and seemingly unconnected pieces of information. Totally unstructured interviewing is rarely used as the sole means of collecting data in qualitative research. In most studies the researcher can combine all three types of interviewing so that some standardized information is obtained, some of the same open-ended questions are asked of all participants, and some time is spent in an unstructured mode so that fresh insights and new information can emerge.

Interviewer and Respondent Interaction

Dexter (1970) says there are three variables in every interview situation that determine the nature of the interaction: "(1) the personality and skill of the interviewer, (2) the attitudes and orientation of the interviewee, and (3) the definition of both (and often by significant others) of the situation" (p. 24). These factors also determine the type of information obtained from an interview. Let us suppose, for example, that two researchers are studying an innovative curriculum for first-year college students. One interviewer (A) is predisposed to innovative practices in general, while the other (B) favors traditional educational practices. One student informant (C) is assigned to the program, while student (D) requests the curriculum and is eager to be interviewed. The particular combination of interviewer and student that evolves will determine, to some extent, the type of data obtained. Thus subjectivity and complexity are inherent in the interview encounter. Dexter (1970, p. 161) rightly observes that "the process of interviewing itself is a social phenomenon, which can profitably be analyzed reflectively."

Although it is impossible to escape the human factor in the interview situation, the interviewer can minimize gross distortion. This means being neutral and nonjudgmental no matter how much a respondent's revelations violate the interviewer's own standards. A good interviewer refrains from arguing, is sensitive to the verbal and nonverbal messages being conveyed, and is a good reflective listener: "Like the therapist, the research interviewer listens more than he talks, and listens with a sympathetic and lively interest. He finds it helpful occasionally to rephrase and reflect back to the informant what he seems to be expressing and to summarize the remarks as a check on understanding" (Whyte, 1982, p. 112).

Obviously, becoming a skilled interviewer takes practice. Indeed, practice combined with feedback on one's performance is the best way to develop the needed skills. Role playing, peer critiquing, videotaping, observing experienced interviewers at work—these are ways novice researchers can improve their performance in this regard.

What makes a good respondent? Anthropologists and sociologists speak of a good respondent as an "informant"—one who understands the culture but is also able to reflect on it and articulate for the researcher what is going on. Key informants are able, to some extent, to adopt the stance of the investigator, thus becoming a valuable guide in unfamiliar territory. Dexter (1970) distinguishes the key informant interview from the elite interview. Elite interviews can be conducted with any person who has "specialized" information—that is, the interviewer is interested in that particular person's definition of the situation.

The respondent need not have a broad understanding of the culture. In its purest form, elite interviews are unstructured. In the final analysis, a good informant is one who can express thoughts, feelings, opinions, his or her *perspective*, on the topic being studied.

Dexter (1970) raises the interesting question of what respondents get out of being interviewed (aside from possible remuneration). It is, he notes, an opportunity for them to tell people something. This in itself is pleasurable and reinforcing. Moreover, some people enjoy the self-analysis, the opportunity to clarify their own thoughts and experiences. Finally, most people are flattered by the interest of a sympathetic listener.

Thus the interviewer/respondent interaction is a complex phenomenon. Both parties bring biases, predispositions, and attitudes that color the interaction and the data elicited. A skilled interviewer accounts for these factors in order to extract worthwhile information. Taking a stance that is nonjudgmental, sensitive, and respectful of the respondent determines the interview's success. As Denzin (1970, p. 142) notes: "While the interviewer is the expert in asking the questions, the respondent is the expert as far as answers are concerned."

Beginning the Interview

Collecting data through interviews involves, first of all, determining whom to interview. For qualitative case studies, the answer depends on what the investigator wants to know and from whose perspective that information is desired. Selecting respondents on the basis of what they can contribute to the researcher's understanding of the phenomenon under study means engaging in purposive or theoretical sampling (discussed in Chapter Three). In a case study of a community school program, for example, a holistic picture of the program would involve the experiences and perceptions of people having different associations with the program—administrators, teachers, students, community residents. In Kline's (1981) case study of a back-to-industry program for postsecondary faculty, it was essential to interview both postsecondary faculty and industry officials. Unlike survey research where the number and representativeness of the sample are major considerations, in this type of research the crucial factor is not the number of respondents but rather the potential of each person to contribute to the development of insight and understanding of the phenomenon.

How does one identify such people? One way is through initial on-site observation of the program, activity, or phenomenon under study. On-site observations often involve informal discussions with participants to discover those who should be interviewed in depth. A second means of locating contacts is to begin with a key person who is considered knowledgeable by others and then ask that person for referrals. Initial informants can be found through the investigator's own personal contacts, through community and private organizations, through advertisements in newspapers or public places, or through random door-to-door or person-to-person contacts. Dexter (1970) warns against being misled by an eager but not particularly helpful informant. He suggests that the interviewer convey the idea that early interviews are part of a preliminary exploration that will lead to identifying key informants. This process can be accelerated by interviewing someone thoroughly familiar with the situation or, conversely, someone who is new enough to the situation to see how it compares to other situations (Denzin, 1970).

Taylor and Bogdan (1984, pp. 87–88) list five issues that should be addressed at the outset of every interview:

1. The investigator's motives and intentions and the inquiry's purpose
2. The protection of respondents through the use of pseudonyms
3. Deciding who has final say over the study's content
4. Payment (if any)
5. Logistics with regard to time, place, and number of interviews to be scheduled

Taylor and Bogdan also suggest several ways of maximizing the time spent getting an informant to share information. A slow-starting interview, for example, can be moved along by asking respondents for basic descriptive information about themselves, the event, or the phenomenon under study. Interviews aimed at constructing life-history case studies can be augmented by written narrative, personal documents, and daily activity logs that informants are asked to submit ahead of time. The value of an interview, of course, depends on the interviewer's knowing enough about the topic to ask meaningful questions in language easily understood by the informant. This, too, is part of the preparation for interviewing.

Asking Good Questions

The key to getting good data from interviewing is to ask good questions. Asking good questions takes practice. An investigator new to collecting data through interviews will feel more confident with a structured interview format where most, if not all, questions are written out ahead of time in the form of an interview schedule. Working from an interview schedule allows the new researcher to gain the experience and confidence needed to conduct open-ended questioning.

Preparing a list of questions in a research study serves two purposes: It is a means of translating the research objectives into specific and perhaps even measurable language; and it is a way of motivating respondents to share their knowledge of the phenomenon under study (Denzin, 1970). A person's knowledge of a topic can range from fact to opinion. Patton (1980) lists six kinds of questions that can be used to get different types of information from respondents:

- *Experience/behavior questions* are "aimed at eliciting descriptions of experiences, behaviors, actions, and activities that would have been observable had the observer been present" (p. 207).
- *Opinion/value questions* try to find out "what people *think* about the world or about a specific program. They tell us people's goals, intentions, desires, and values" (p. 207).
- *Feeling questions* are "aimed at understanding the emotional response of people to their experiences and thoughts" (p. 207).

- *Knowledge questions* find out what a respondent considers to be factual information regarding the research topic.
- *Sensory questions* determine what sensory stimuli—sight, sound, touch, taste, or smell—respondents are sensitive to.
- *Background/demographic questions* "locate the respondent in relation to other people. Age, education, race, residence/mobility questions, and the like are standard background questions" (p. 209).

The way in which questions are worded is a crucial consideration in extracting the type of information desired. An obvious place to begin is making certain that what is being asked is clear to the person being interviewed. Questions need to be understood in familiar language: "Using words that make sense to the interviewee, words that reflect the respondent's world view, will improve the quality of data obtained during the interview. In many cases, without sensitivity to the impact of particular words on the person being interviewed, the answer may make no sense at all—or there may be no answer" (Patton, 1980, p. 227).

Besides being careful to word questions in language clear to the respondent, the interviewer must be aware of his or her stance. Patton (1980) suggests that the interviewer assume a "presuppositional" stance—that is, he or she presupposes that the respondent has something to contribute, has had an experience worth talking about, and has an opinion of interest to the researcher. An interviewer should also assume neutrality with regard to the respondent's knowledge. Patton (1980, p. 231) distinguishes neutrality from rapport: "At the same time that I am neutral with regard to the *content* of what is being said to me, I care very much that that person is willing to share with me what they are saying. *Rapport is a stance vis-à-vis the person being interviewed. Neutrality is a stance vis-à-vis the content of what that person says.*"

There are several types of questions an interviewer can ask to stimulate response from an informant. Strauss, Schatzman, Bucher, and Sabshin (1981) offer a list of four major categories of questions: hypothetical questions, devil's advocate questions, ideal position questions, and interpretive questions. Each is defined in Table 4 and illustrated with examples from a

**Table 4. Four Types of Questions with Examples
from a JTPA Training Program Case Study.**

Type of Question	Example
• Hypothetical Question: asks what the respondent might do or what it might be like in a particular situation; it usually begins with "what if" or "suppose"	"Suppose it is my first day in this training program. What would it be like?"
• Devil's Advocate Question: challenges the respondent to consider an opposing view	"Some people would say that employees who lose their job did something to bring it about. What would you say to them?"
• Ideal Position Question: asks the respondent to describe an ideal situation	"What do you think the ideal training program would be like?"
• Interpretive Question: advances tentative interpretation of what the respondent has been saying and asks for a reaction	"Would you say that returning to school as an adult is different from what you expected?"

case study of displaced workers participating in a Job Training and Partnership (JTPA) program.

Some types of questions should be avoided in an interview. Avoid multiple questions—either one question that is actually a double question or a series of single questions that does not allow the respondent a chance to answer one by one. An example of a double question is: "How do you feel about the staff and the courses in this training program?" Patton (1980, p. 229), although admitting that other researchers might not agree, recommends avoiding "why" questions. Not only do such questions lead to difficulty in making causal inferences, but they may lead to an infinite regression of why, why, why. Leading questions should also be avoided. These set the respondent up to accept the researcher's point of view. The question "What emotional problems have you had since losing your job?" reflects a bias suggesting that anyone losing a job will have emotional problems. Finally, all researchers warn against asking yes/no questions. Any question that can be answered with a simple yes or no probably will be too simple to have value.

In summary, then, questions are at the heart of interviewing, and to collect meaningful data one must ask good questions. Determining the type of information desired—opinion, experience, feeling, knowledge, sensory, or demographic—aids in deciding what type of question to ask. To unlock the "internal perspectives of every interviewee" (Patton, 1980, p. 253), the interviewer can make use of hypothetical, devil's advocate, ideal position, and interpretive questions.

Recording and Evaluating Interview Data

There are three basic ways to record interview data. The most common method by far is to tape-record the interview. This practice ensures that everything said is preserved for analysis. The interviewer can also listen for ways to improve his or her questioning technique. Malfunctioning equipment and a respondent's uneasiness with being recorded are the drawbacks. Most researchers find, however, that after some initial wariness respondents tend to forget they are being taped. Occasionally interviews are videotaped. This practice allows for recording of nonverbal behavior, but it is also more cumbersome and intrusive than tape-recording the interview.

A second way to record interview data is to take notes during the interview. Since not everything said can be recorded and since at the outset of a study a researcher is not certain what is important enough to write down, this method is recommended only when mechanical recording is not feasible. Some investigators like to take written notes in addition to taping the session. The interviewer may want to record his or her reactions to something the informant says, to signal the informant of the importance of what is being said, or to pace the interview.

The third—and least desirable—way to record interview data is to write down as much as can be remembered as soon after the interview as possible. The problems with this method are obvious, but there are times when writing or recording during an interview might be intrusive (interviewing terminally ill patients, for example). In any case, researchers must write their reflections immediately following the interview. These reflections might contain insights suggested by the interview, descriptive notes on the behavior, verbal and nonverbal, of the informant, parenthet-

ical thoughts of the researcher, and so on. Postinterview notes
allow the investigator to monitor the process of data collection
as well as begin to analyze the information itself.

Ideally, verbatim transcription of recorded interviews provides the best data base for analysis. Exhibit 1 presents excerpts
from a transcribed interview conducted as part of a study of
consortia of higher education that had failed. Many researchers,
however, find transcribing interviews to be prohibitively expensive and time-consuming. An alternative to verbatim transcription
is the *interview log*. This system was developed by the author as
a result of supervising graduate students who can rarely afford

Exhibit 1. Sample Interview from a Case Study of
Failed Consortia of Higher Education.

Interviewer (I):   The first question I have is about the mission of [name
of consortium]. My understanding is that it had three general areas in
terms of mission: (1) the production of courses and materials for
learning at a distance, (2) the promotion of external degree programs,
and (3) the development of research on the adult learner and learning
at a distance. Does that agree with your perceptions of [name of con-
sortium]?

Respondent (R):   I think that was what they were trying to do. Now the
extent to which they accomplished it is something else, but I do agree
that that is what they were trying to do. It was an offshoot of some
experiment in [state] but, in general, I would agree that that is what
they were trying to do.

I: From your perspective, what were the significant accomplishments
of [name of consortium]?

R: I think they did produce some very good programs. Very few, but
what they did produce were top quality and they did try to help the
cooperating universities set up the programs in the states. For instance, we had a State Coordinator located at [another institution]
and she represented both her institution and our own in setting up
learning centers for the state. I suspect we never would have done
that without the financial assistance of [the consortium] at the very
beginning.

I: What are the learning centers you referred to?

R: Places where students could go to take examinations or view the television programs if they had missed them. These were primarily in
[another institution's] extension facilities but there were expenses
involved and [the consortium] provided funding for them. We still
have them and they never would have been started had it not been
for [the consortium] so that is a real plus.

I: So, in other words, if I am hearing you correctly, [the consortium]

Exhibit 1. Sample Interview from a Case Study of
Failed Consortia of Higher Education, Cont'd.

served as sort of a catalyst for certain activities that have continued since its demise?

R: Yes.

I: What were the shortcomings of [the consortium]?

R: I think that their ideas were too grandiose. No real funding base that they could count on and the fact that their desire to develop good programs, and they were very good . . . they spent too much money! Now, presumably they couldn't have developed the good programs if they hadn't spent all this money. But I think so much money was spent on the programming that anything else they might have done just couldn't be done.

I: So was the focus too much on . . .

R: Production, yeah. . . .

I: Why do you think [the consortium] was ultimately terminated?

R: Well, for one thing the leadership, but also the funding. I think when [name] tried to . . . the last straw was when he tried to turn it into a competing institution.

I: The transition to [name of] University?

R: Yeah, and people saw that as a possible threat.

I: How did [the consortium] transform into [name of] University?

R: I don't know, but I would suspect originally with [name]. Now I've not gone through these files that you have access to and there may be some indication there. I think that when [name] took over . . . well, before he took over, people weren't that hot on [the consortium] but they weren't unduly opposed to it. But he started changing it and it seemed to a lot of us anyway that he was trying to change it to something that was not what we were interested in.

I: Are there any things about the leadership that you can tell me specifically that may have contributed to the termination of [the consortium]?

R: I think if a person that is in charge of an organization does not realize, particularly when it's composed of a number of other organizations, if he does not realize we all have an equal say in it . . . if he thinks "I'm going to do something and I don't give a damn about what the member institutions want," it's going to fail because ultimately the leader, unless he or she has a complacent group of member institutions, can't do anything. And it may not be overt clashing; it may be foot-dragging. There are all sorts of ways to express your displeasure and because sometimes. . . . But [name] is a very interesting person. When he was at [institution] he tried to do some very interesting and innovative things, but somehow it didn't work. He's brilliant but that's not always enough. You have to know how to work with people. And if you have a really good idea, you'd better sell it to the people before you go outside and announce it.

Source: Offerman (1985). Reprinted with permission.

to transcribe interview tapes. The researcher begins by identifying at the top of a legal-sized pad the name, date, and other necessary details of the interview. The interviewer/researcher then plays the tape and takes notes on important statements or ideas expressed by the informant. Words or phrases or entire sentences are quoted exactly. These notes are coded to the tape counter so the exact location of such words can be accessed quickly at a later time. Tape position is recorded to the left of the words or phrases the researcher deems important. In a column to the far right is space for the researcher to add his or her own observations about what was said. The data on the interview log can later be coded according to the emerging themes or categories from the data analysis phase of the study. (Strategies for analyzing qualitative data are covered in Chapter Eight.) Exhibit 2 is a sample interview log using the same interview data found in Exhibit 1. Rather than transcribing the interview verbatim, however, the log captures the main points. Noting the tape position allows the researcher to access the original data quickly.

In addition to recording interview data for analysis, it is important to assess, as best as possible, the *quality* of the data obtained. Several factors may influence an informant's responses, factors that may be difficult for the researcher to discern. The informant's health, mood at the time of interview, and so on may affect the quality of data obtained, as might an informant's ulterior motives for participating in the project (Whyte, 1982). Furthermore, all information obtained from an informant has been selected, either consciously or unconsciously, from all that he or she knows. What you get in an interview is simply the informant's *perception.*

This personal perspective is, of course, what is sought in qualitative research. There is the possibility that information has been distorted or exaggerated. Such distortation can be detected by checking the plausibility of the account and the reliability of the informant (Whyte, 1982). "The major way to detect and correct distortion," according to Whyte, "is by *comparing an informant's account with accounts given by other informants"* (p. 116). One might also confirm the informant's account by

Exhibit 2. Sample Interview Log Using Interview in Exhibit 1.

Interviewee #8
Name of Consortium
Male, Dean of Continuing Education

Tape Position	Respondent's Comments	Researcher's Notes
074	Agrees tried to carry out three-part mission	—
093	"Very few," but some top-quality programs; learning centers, persons, finances	Importance of people and financing in establishment of programs
109	Describes learning centers; "still have them"—"a real plus"	Some programs continue despite end of consortium
117	—	Consortium as catalyst
125	Ideas "too grandiose," "spent too much money," "no real funding base"	Funding is a crucial problem
134	"Production" focus	—
144	Funding as well as leadership reasons for termination; "he tried to turn it into a competing institution"	Leadership important—can't become a "competing institution"
169	Change in focus created problem	Importance of individual administrator
179	Leadership problem: "you have to know how to work with people"; must consider member institutions	Leadership qualities needed in consortium

checking documentary material or directly observing the situation.

Summary

In qualitative case studies, interviewing is a major source of qualitative data needed for understanding the phenomenon under study. Interviews can range in structure from those, on the one hand, in which questions and the order in which they are asked are predetermined to, on the other hand, totally unstructured interviews in which nothing is set ahead of time. Most common is the semistructured interview that is guided by a set of questions and issues to be explored, but neither the exact wording nor the order of questions is predetermined.

The success of an interview depends on the interaction between interviewer and respondent. To a large extent, this interaction is contingent upon the researcher's demeanor and his or her skill in asking questions. The researcher should have a clear notion of the type of information desired so that an appropriate questioning strategy can be used. Special care should also be devoted to recording the data gathered and evaluating its authenticity. An interview log is a useful substitute for verbatim transcription.

Interviewing, especially semistructured and unstructured formats, fares well when compared to other data collection techniques in terms of the validity of the information obtained. There is ample opportunity to probe for clarification and ask questions appropriate to the respondent's knowledge, involvement, and status. The interview also provides for "continuous assessment and evaluation of information by the inquirer, allowing him to redirect, probe, and summarize" (Guba and Lincoln, 1981, p. 187).

Interviewing, like any other data collection technique, has its strengths and its limitations. The researcher who attends to the limitations while maximizing the strengths inherent in all phases of the interview process will be richly rewarded by the data obtained. For the interview is the best way—and perhaps the only way—to find out "what is in and on someone else's mind" (Patton, 1980, p. 196).

CHAPTER 6

Being a Careful
Observer

Interviews are a primary source of data in doing case study research; so too are observations. Collecting data from observing
phenomena of interest is commonly referred to as participant
observation. It can be distinguished from interviewing in two
ways: First, interviewing occurs in a place designated for that
purpose versus the natural field setting of participant observation; second, interview data represent a secondhand account of
the world versus the firsthand experience of observing (Taylor
and Bogdan, 1984). In the real world of collecting data, however, informal interviews and conversations are often interwoven with observation. The terms *fieldwork* and *field study*
usually connote both activities (observation and interviews)
and, to a lesser degree, documentary analysis. That caveat not-
withstanding, the primary focus of this chapter is on the activity of *observation:* observation as a research tool, what to observe, the relationship between observer and observed, and
recording observations.

Observation in Research

Just as casually conversing with someone differs from interviewing, so too does routine observation differ from research

observation. Observation is a research tool when it "(1) serves a formulated research purpose, (2) is planned deliberately, (3) is recorded systematically, and (4) is subjected to checks and controls on validity and reliability" (Kidder, 1981b, p. 264).

Critics of participant observation as a data-gathering technique point to the highly subjective and therefore unreliable nature of human perception. As with any other data collection technique, however, one needs to be trained in its usage. Patton (1980) writes that "experiments and simulations that document the inaccuracy of spontaneous observations made by untrained and unprepared observers are no more indicative of the potential quality of observation than an amateur community talent show is indicative of what professional performers do" (p. 123). Training to be a skilled observer includes "learning how to write descriptively; practicing the disciplined recording of field notes; knowing how to separate detail from trivia . . . and using rigorous methods to validate observations" (Patton, 1980, p. 123). In a discussion of training observers to gather specific information through the use of codes or other devices, Reid (1982) suggests using film, videotapes or audiotapes, and role playing. The best way to learn how to observe, according to Guba and Lincoln (1981), is to become apprenticed to someone experienced in this technique. One might also read other people's accounts of the experience.

There are numerous reasons why an investigator might want to gather data through observation. As an outsider an observer will notice things that have become routine to the participants themselves, things which may lead to understanding the context. The participant observer gets to see things firsthand and to use his or her own knowledge and expertise in interpreting what is observed, rather than relying upon once-removed accounts from interviewers. Selltiz, Jahoda, Deutsch, and Cook (1959, p. 201) comment on this point: "The degree to which one can predict behavior from interview data is at best limited, and the gap between the two can be quite large. In contrast, observational techniques yield data that pertain directly to typical behavioral situations." Observation makes it possible to record behavior as it is happening. Finally, there are topics people may not feel free to talk about or may not want to discuss. In studying a small educational unit, for example, the researcher might observe dissension and strife among certain staff members that an interview would not reveal. Observation is the best technique to use when an activity, event, or situation can be observed first-hand, when a fresh perspective is desired, or when participants are not able or willing to discuss the topic under study.

What to Observe?

What to observe is determined by several factors. The most important is one's purpose in conducting the study in the first place—that is, the conceptual framework, the problem, or the questions of interest determine what is to be observed. As noted in Chapter Four, one's disciplinary orientation often determines how the problem is defined. An educator might observe a school because of an interest in how students learn, whereas a sociologist might visit the same school because of an interest in social institutions. Practical considerations also play a part in determining what to observe. Certain behavior is difficult to observe; one has to have the time, money, and energy to devote to observation; and one has to be *allowed* to observe by those in the situation of interest. Hawkins (1982, p. 22) notes that "impressions also influence the choice of what to observe. Researchers often begin a series of investigations by impressionistic, informal observation." These early impressions help determine subsequent patterns of observation. Goetz and LeCompte (1984, p. 112) write that what to observe depends on the topic, the conceptual framework, "the data that begin to emerge as the ethnographer interacts in the daily flow of events and activities, and the intuitive reactions and hunches that ethnographers experience as these factors coalesce."

What to observe is somewhat a function of how structured the observer wants to be. Just as there is a range of structure in interviewing, there is also a range of structure in observation. One can decide ahead of time to concentrate on observing certain events, behavior, or persons. A code sheet might be used to record instances of specified behavior. Less structured observations can be compared to a television camera scanning the area. Where one begins looking depends on the research question, but where to focus or stop action cannot be determined ahead of time. The focus must be allowed to emerge and in fact may change over the course of the study.

Nevertheless, one cannot observe *everything* and one must start somewhere. Several writers (Selltiz, Jahoda, Deutsch, and Cook, 1959; Goetz and LeCompte, 1984; Patton, 1980; Taylor and Bogdan, 1984) present lists of things to observe, at least to get started in the activity. Here is a checklist of elements likely to be present in an observation:

1. *The setting:* What is the physical environment like? What is the context? What kinds of behavior does the setting "encourage, permit, discourage, or prevent" (Selltiz, Jahoda, Deutsch, and Cook, 1959, p. 209)? The principal's office, the school bus, the cafeteria, and the classroom vary in physical attributes as well as in anticipated behavior.
2. *The participants:* Describe who is in the scene, how many people, and their roles. What brings these people together? Who is allowed here?
3. *Activities and interactions:* What is going on? Is there a definable sequence of activities? How do the people interact with the activity and with one another? How are people and activities "connected or interrelated—either from the participants' point of view or from the researcher's perspective" (Goetz and LeCompte, 1984, p. 113)?
4. *Frequency and duration:* When did the situation begin? How long does it last? "Is it a recurring type of situation, or unique? If it recurs, how frequently? What are the occasions that give rise to it? How typical of such situations is the one being observed" (Selltiz, Jahoda, Deutsch, and Cook, 1959, p. 210)?
5. *Subtle factors:* Less obvious but perhaps as important to the observation are:
    *   Informal and unplanned activities
    *   Symbolic and connotative meanings of words
    *   Nonverbal communication such as dress and physical space

- Unobtrusive measures such as physical clues
- What does *not* happen—especially if it ought to have happened (Patton, 1980, p. 155)

Each participant observation experience has its own rhythm and flow. The duration of a single observation or the total amount of time spent collecting data in this way is a function of the problem being investigated. There is no ideal amount of time to spend observing nor is there one preferred pattern of observation. For some situations, observation over an extended period of time may be most appropriate; for others, shorter periodic observations make the most sense given the purpose of the study and practical constraints.

The process of collecting data through observations can be broken into the three stages of entry, data collection, and exit. Gaining entry into a site begins with gaining the confidence and permission of those who can approve the activity. This step is more easily accomplished through a mutual contact who can recommend the researcher to the "gatekeepers" involved. Once entry has been gained, Taylor and Bogdan (1984) have some comments for the first few days in the field:

- Observers should be relatively passive and unobtrusive, put people at ease, learn how to act and dress in the setting.
- Collecting data is secondary to becoming familiar with the setting.
- Keep the first observations fairly short to avoid becoming overwhelmed with the novelty of the situation.
- Be honest but not overly technical or detailed in explaining what you are doing.

They also suggest that the researcher establish rapport by paying homage to the participants' routines, establishing what the observer has in common with the participants, helping out on occasion, being humble, and showing interest in the activity.

Once one has become familiar with the setting and begins to see what is there to observe, serious data collection can begin. There is little glamour and much hard work in this phase of research. It takes great concentration to observe intently, re-

member as much as possible, and then record, in as much detail
as possible, what one has observed. Patton (1980, p. 184) comments on this phase of fieldwork: "The dominant motifs in
fieldwork are hard work, enormous discipline, and concentration on the mundane, often to the point of boredom. . . . Alas,
let the truth be told: The gathering of field data involves very little glory and an abundance of nose-to-the-grindstone drudgery."

The overall time spent on the site, the number of visits,
and the number of observations made per visit cannot be precisely determined ahead of time. There will come a point when
time and money run out and one begins to realize that no new
information is being uncovered. Ideally, depletion of resources
coincides with saturation of information. Leaving the field,
however, may be even more difficult than gaining entry. It may
mean "breaking attachments and sometimes even offending
those one has studied, leaving them feeling betrayed and used"
(Taylor and Bogdan, 1984, p. 67). Taylor and Bogdan recommend easing out or drifting off—that is, "gradually cutting
down on the frequency of visits and letting people know that
the research is coming to an end" (p. 68).

Relationship Between Observer and Observed

There are several stances one can assume while collecting
information as an observer. These range from being a full participant—the investigator is a member of the group being observed
—to being a spectator. Junker (1960) delineates the possible
stances as:

1. *Complete participant:* The researcher is a member of
the group being studied and conceals his or her observer role
from the group. The inside information one can obtain by using
this method must be weighed against the possible disadvantages
—loss of perspective on the group, being labeled a spy or traitor
when research activities are revealed, and the questionable ethics of deceiving the other participants.

2. *Participant as observer:* The researcher's observer activities, which are known to the group, are subordinate to the
researcher's role as a participant. The tradeoff here is between

the depth of the information revealed to the researcher and the level of confidentiality promised to the group in order to obtain this information. These issues have a large influence on the results of the case study and the researcher's report.

3. *Observer as participant:* The researcher's observer activities are known to the group and are "more or less publicly sponsored by [the] people in the situation [being] studied" (Junker, 1960, p. 37). The researcher's participation in the group is definitely secondary to his or her role of information gatherer. Using this method, one may have access to many people and a wide range of information, but the level of the information revealed is controlled by the group members being investigated.

4. *Complete observer:* The researcher is either hidden from the group (for example, behind a one-way mirror) or in a completely public setting such as an airport or library.

Inherent in this continuum is the extent to which the investigation is overt or covert (Guba and Lincoln, 1981). Whether one is a complete participant or a complete observer, the "real" activity is not known to those being observed. This situation leads to ethical questions related to the privacy and protection of research subjects. These issues are discussed more fully in Chapter Ten.

In reality, case study researchers are rarely total participants or total observers. Rather, they are what Gans (1982, p. 54) calls a *researcher participant*—one "who participates in a social situation but is personally only partially involved, so that he can function as a researcher." Although the ideal in qualitative case studies is to get inside the perspective of the participants, full participation is not always possible. A researcher can never know exactly how it feels to be illiterate or mentally ill, for example. A question can also be raised as to just how much better it is to be an insider. Being born into a group, "going native," or just being a member does not necessarily afford the perspective necessary for studying the phenomenon. Jarvie (1982, p. 68) notes that "there is nothing especially privileged about the observation of a parade made by those in it. Spectators are in a better position; television viewers in a still better one." On the other hand, Swisher (1986) was able to get reliable information about multicultural education from parents and teachers in a reservation community because she herself is a member of the community. Patton (1980) underscores the balance needed between insider and outsider in qualitative research: "Experiencing the program as an insider is what necessitates the *participant* part of participant observation. At the same time, however, there is clearly an *observer* side to this process. The challenge is to combine participation and observation so as to become capable of understanding the program as an insider while describing the program for outsiders" (p. 128).

As the researcher gains familiarity with the case—whether it is a program, a person, or an event—the mix of participation and observation is likely to change. One might begin as a spectator and gradually become involved in the activities being observed. In other situations an investigator might decide to begin "as a complete participant in order to experience what it is like to be initially immersed in the program and then gradually withdraw participation over the period of study until finally taking the role of occasional observer" (Patton, 1980, p. 127). In recounting her field experiences in a home for the aged, Posner (1980) traces her movement from participant observer as a volunteer worker, to complete participant as a programmer, to observer with minimum participation.

Participant observation is a schizophrenic activity in that one usually participates but not to the extent of becoming totally absorbed in the activity. At the same time one is participating, one is trying to stay sufficiently detached to observe and analyze. It is a marginal position and personally difficult to sustain. Gans (1982) captures the distress in being a researcher participant: "The temptation to become involved was ever-present. I had to fight the urge to shed the emotional handcuffs that bind the researcher, and to react spontaneously to the situation, to relate to people as a person and to derive pleasure rather than data from the situation. Often, I carried on an internal tug of war, to decide how much spontaneous participation was possible without missing something as a researcher" (p. 54).

The ambiguity of participant observation is one source of

anxiety for the qualitative researcher. Gans cites three other sources that make this method of gathering data particularly difficult. There is, he writes, "the constant worry about the flow of research activities." And he goes on to ask: "Is one doing the right thing at the right time, attending the right meeting, or talking to the right people" (p. 58)? Another source of anxiety is "how to make sense out of what one is studying, how not to be upset by the initial inability to understand and how to order the constant influx of data" (p. 59). Finally, the inherent deception in participant observation leads to "a pervasive feeling of guilt" and "a tendency to overidentify with the people being studied" (p. 59).

Another concern has been raised recently: the extent to which the observer-investigator affects that which is being observed. Ideally, the researcher is a neutral figure who "does not change the situation in any way that might affect the data" (Bogdan, 1972, p. 21). In reality, though, the question is not *whether* the process of observing affects what is observed but rather "how to monitor those effects and take them into consideration when interpreting data" (Patton, 1980, p. 189). In a discussion of the reactive effects of direct, structured observations, Kazdin (1982) offers three explanations why the activities of those being observed might be altered: If participants are apprehensive about being judged, they may respond in socially desirable ways; if participants are aware of being assessed, they may behave in response to the assessment conditions; and, finally, participants may regulate their behavior from feedback obtained from observers—as when notes are taken or behavior is attended to in a particular fashion. Of course, "the more controlled the research, the farther it departs from natural interaction, the greater the likelihood that one will end up studying the effects of research procedures" (Taylor and Bogdan, 1984, p. 47).

The extent to which an observer actually changes the situation studied is not at all clear. Frankenberg (1982, p. 51) points out that in traditional anthropological studies the activities of an ethnographer (researcher) are not likely to change "custom and practice built up over years." It is more likely that the researcher will prove to be "a catalyst for changes that are already taking place." Others have suggested that the stability of a social setting is rarely disrupted by the presence of an observer (Reinharz, 1979). In any case, the researcher must be sensitive to the effects one might be having on the situation and accounting for those effects. Patton (1980) points out that observer/observed is an interdependent relationship in which the researcher too may be changed as a result of the interaction. Indeed, it is this interdependence that "gives naturalistic inquiry its perspective" (p. 192).

Recording Observations

What is written down or mechanically recorded from a period of observation becomes the raw data from which a study's findings eventually emerge. The more complete the recording, the easier it is to analyze the data. How much can one record during an observation? The answer depends on the researcher's role and the extent to which he or she is a participant in the activity. On-site recording can thus range from continuous (especially if one is a total observer), to taking sketchy notes, to not recording anything at all during an observation. Although mechanical devices such as videotapes, film, or tape recorders can be used to record observations, the cost and obtrusiveness of these methods often preclude their use. It is much more likely that a researcher will jot down a few notes during an observation or wait until afterward to record what has been observed. Thus, unlike an interviewer who can usually fall back on a tape recording of the session, a participant observer has to rely on his or her memory to recount the session.

Even if the researcher has been able to take a few notes during an observation, it is imperative that full notes be written, typed, or dictated as soon after the observation as possible. It takes great self-discipline to sit down and describe what one has observed. The observation itself is only half the work: "For the actual writing of notes may take as long or longer than did the observation! Indeed, a reasonable rule of thumb here is to expect and plan to spend as much time writing notes as one spent

observing. . . . All the fun of actually being out and about mon-
keying around in some setting must also be met by cloistered
rigor in committing to paper—and therefore to future usefulness
—what has taken place" (Lofland, 1971, pp. 103–104).

Every researcher devises his or her own technique for remembering and recording the specifics of an observation. It can
be an intimidating part of qualitative research, however, and
one is advised to begin with short periods of observation and
then practice recalling and recording data. Taylor and Bogdan
(1984) offer numerous suggestions for recalling data. Later recall will be helped if *during* an observation investigators:

- Pay attention.
- Shift from a "wide angle" to a "narrow angle" lens—that is,
  focusing "on a specific person, interaction, or activity, while
  mentally blocking out all the others" (p. 54).
- Look for key words in people's remarks that will stand out
  later.
- Concentrate on the first and last remarks in each conversation.
- Mentally play back remarks and scenes during breaks in the
  talking or observing.

Once the observation is completed, they suggest leaving
the setting as soon as observing as much as can be remembered;
recording field notes as soon as possible after observing; in case
of a time lag between observing and recording, summarizing or
outlining the observation; drawing a diagram of the setting and
tracing movements through it; and incorporating pieces of data
remembered at later times into the original field notes (Taylor
and Bogdan, 1984). Bogdan (1972) also advises against talking
to anyone about the observation before notes have been recorded. Finally, he suggests being more concerned with remembering the substance of a conversation than with producing a
"flawless verbatim reproduction" (p. 42).

Field notes based on observation need to be in a format
that will allow the researcher to find the desired information easily. Formats vary, but a set of notes usually begins with the time,

place, and purpose of the observation. It is also helpful to list the participants present or at least to indicate how many and what kinds of people are present—described in ways meaningful to the research. If the researcher is observing a school board meeting about a recent racial incident, for example, she or he could note the number of people present, whether they are parents, teachers, board members, or interested community residents, and their racial makeup. A diagram of the setting's physical aspects might be included. Other hints suggested by Taylor and Bogdan (1984) for setting up field notes is to leave wide margins for later notes, form new paragraphs often for ease of reading and data analysis, and use quotation marks to indicate direct quotes.

The actual content of field notes usually includes the following:

- Verbal descriptions of the setting, the people, the activities.
- Direct quotations or at least the substance of what people said.
- Observer's comments—put in the margins or in the running narrative and identified by underlining, bracketing, or the initials "OC." Observer's comments can include the researcher's feelings, reactions, hunches, initial interpretations, and working hypotheses.

Exhibit 3 presents an excerpt from field notes written after the researcher observed a class session. The investigator was particularly interested in instruction and in the interaction between teacher and students. The topic for this session was the development and use of overhead transparencies. Note the observer's comments interwoven throughout the recording.

Ethnographers often separate the observer's comments from the narrative account of the observation through the use of a fieldwork journal. This journal is an introspective record of the anthropologist's experience in the field. It includes his or her ideas, fears, mistakes, confusion, reactions to the experience. In addition to the narrative account and the fieldwork journal, ethnographers often write memos or "think papers" containing analysis and interpretation (Spradley, 1979). Case

Exhibit 3. Sample of Field Notes (Excerpts).

I got to the classroom about 10 minutes early so that I could observe how the classroom was laid out. I took a seat in the back and sketched a diagram of the class. There were still 5 minutes to go and no one had showed up yet, so I went out into the hall to wait for B. After a minute or so, B came along. I saw that B didn't have any materials and when I asked about it, B indicated that all the things needed were already in the classroom. We went in together. Only one student had arrived, but there were still a few minutes to go.

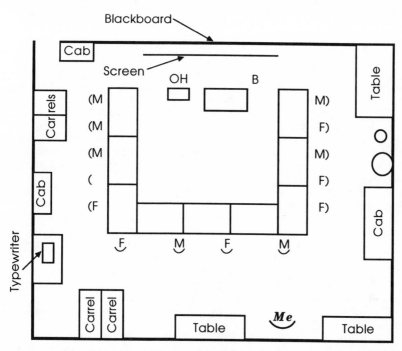

Another student arrived and started to chat about the first student's teaching activity that had taken place the day before. As they talked a few more students arrived, one of whom joined in the conversation. A few more students arrived. B was in the front of the classroom waiting to start the class. The conversation got onto the topic of lesson plans and the male in front of me asked what a lesson plan was. B asked him if he had gotten the handout on the topic, and after looking through his books, he said that he hadn't. B would get him a copy during the break. After noting that the class was small today, B asked if they had all picked a topic for the sample lesson that they would have to prepare materials for. Some in-

(continued on next page)

Exhibit 3. Sample of Field Notes (Excerpts), Cont'd.

dicated that they hadn't, and B asked them, "What are you interested in?" B told them that they would talk about it during lab time. Another student arrived. B asked the class again if anyone else had picked a topic. A student replied that she would teach multiplication.

B said that the class was going to start. The students quieted down and looked at her as she announced that the subject of today's lesson was going to be how to make overhead transparencies. B asked, "Has anyone ever made an overhead transparency?" A few students indicated that they had, but when they were questioned further on the topic, it turned out that one student had used them but had never made them, and the other had written on some acetate that she then used as an overhead.

B then told the class that this was B's favorite topic because this was a really good, low-cost method that teachers could use to convey complex information to a class. A little effort could go a long way, and they weren't expensive to make. There are a few ways to make them and there are lots of ways to use them. The students who were in marketing were told that transparencies were used a lot in business to support presentations.

B told the class that transparencies were very good in helping to get a message across. They were reminded that this is how their projects would be graded, in how well the overhead helped to convey a message that supported an objective, in what domain of knowledge they would be used, and what the message was.

OC—Up until this time, no one had asked any questions. The students were quiet; they didn't move in their chairs very much. While this was going on, the last of the students who would be attending the session arrived.

The class was asked what a domain was. A student replied, "Cognitive, affective, psychomotor." "Very good," B replied.

"What is a message?" B asked. No reply this time.

B turned on the overhead projector and proceeded to show some examples. The first one was a colorful slide of the planets.

OC—B must like planets. There is a model of the solar system, in similar colors, in B's office.

B pointed out that this particular slide would be useful in having students identify the planets and that the slide would not be very helpful in explaining planetary motion. The students were also shown an example of masking. (The names of the planets were masked by pieces of cardboard so that they could be revealed by the teacher, as required.)

OC—The students were attentive, but quiet, too quiet I thought. What's happening here is that the teacher is not asking enough questions. For example, B could have asked the students what the flaps were for, and why would you want to do such a thing. Instead of telling what the slide was good for, asking what it would be good for. Nice locus of control issue.

The second transparency's subject was the water cycle, a slide consisting of the main and two overlays. B explained how an overhead of this kind could be used to describe a process.

Exhibit 3. Sample of Field Notes (Excerpts), Cont'd.

OC—The students were quiet, no questions.

The next transparency was used to describe a concept, in this case formal and informal balance. B explained that a slide should not be overly cluttered, which brought up the next example, a slide that had too much information on it. B next put up a slide that showed a computer, some modems, and a telephone and asked what the students thought of it. A few students replied that they did not understand it, whereupon B explained that it was a slide showing the electronic bulletin board for the college.

OC—It was probably B's intent to show the class a professional-looking slide, which it was. The content of the slide was, however, out of the experience of the students. This problem might have been gotten around by first explaining the content, and then asking the students what else they might have noticed about the slide, in order to bring up the subject of its professional look.

B asked the class to turn to page 23 of the workbook in order to see what the assignment for overhead transparencies will be. Each student was to make three transparencies relating to a lesson that had been devised by the student. They were to make one with the direct dye medium (the one with the notch), the second with the transfer sheet medium, and the third to be hand-drawn. The slides set would also have to demonstrate the techniques of masking, overlay, and color.

A student asked, "What's masking?" B then explained the concept of slow or controlled revelation. It was explained to the class that this technique is used when you don't wish to show the whole slide at once.

OC—It would have been nice to explain the relationship between masking and overlays.

B passed around a handout that described several techniques for building overheads with masking. B then asked the class if they would like a demonstration of how to make a slide using overlays. B had removed the overhead showing the requirements for the project.

A student asked, "What comes after masking?" B replied, "The use of color."

B then started to show the class the technique for making a slide with two overlays. The slide that showed the water cycle was the subject. The main transparency was made and attached to the frame on all four sides with masking tape. The overlays were then made and attached to the frame on one side only. In B's example, the main was in red and the overlays in blue. B then went on to demonstrate how pieces of different-colored acetate may be used to add color to the slides. B indicated that these materials may be purchased in stores.

OC—No one asks where.

A student asked if the overlays need to be the same color. B replied that they can be anything the student wants.

Source: Brandt (1987). Reprinted with permission.

study researchers are more likely to use the integrated format described above, although some do keep a separate journal of the experience. This itself becomes a data source and is sometimes used to write about the methodology. In a case study of a junior college that had received federal development funds, Malcolm (Malcolm and Welch, 1981) uses his own observer comments to describe his experiences with the methodology. On his first day on the site, he wrote, "in anguish," on the back of a page of notes: "The memory load is tremendous! Recalling people and names, building layout and function, dialogue and argument. I had been afraid of my inability to observe and listen; but that problem, at least on this first day, pales in the face of memory load" (p. 75). Later, in a personal reaction to the methodology, he writes: "Despite intensive preparation for the study, I was surprised by a number of my reactions to the methodology. One was my conviction about the accuracy and validity of the results. . . . Other unexpected reactions related to the tremendous memory load and the constant demand to record the manifold aspects of each observation session, interview, and experience" (Malcolm and Welch, 1981, pp. 67–68).

Summary

Participant observation is a major means of collecting data in case study research. It gives a firsthand account of the situation under study and, when combined with interviewing and document analysis, allows for a holistic interpretation of the phenomenon being investigated. It is the technique of choice when behavior can be observed firsthand or when people cannot or will not discuss the research topic.

Fieldwork, as participant observation is often called, involves going to the site, program, institution, setting—the field— to observe the phenomenon under study. Unless it is public behavior one wants to observe, entry must first be gained from those in authority. Initial times in the field are followed by an intensive period of data collection. The final phase of fieldwork involves leaving gracefully. While on the site, one is absorbed by what to observe, what to remember, what to record. There are guidelines for these activities, but ultimately the success of participant observation rests on the talent and skill of the investigator.

Participant observation maximizes the advantages of the human being as instrument. One relies totally upon one's sensitivity, one's "ability to grasp motives, beliefs, concerns, interests, unconscious behaviors, customs, and the like," and upon tacit as well as propositional knowledge (Guba and Lincoln, 1981, p. 193). The human instrument is capable of understanding the complexity of human interaction encountered in even the shortest of observations. Like any other data collection instrument, the human instrument can be refined, through training, to be attentive and responsive to data gathered through this method.

Even so, there may be problems with the data one collects. Most acute are the biases an investigator brings to the situation. These biases, inherent in all investigations, affect how data are seen, recorded, and interpreted. An observer cannot help but affect and be affected by the setting, and this interaction may lead to a distortion of the real situation. Finally, the schizophrenic aspect of being at once participant and observer is a by-product of this method of data collection not easily dealt with.

Overall, however, there is no substitute for the participant observer. As Guba and Lincoln (1981, p. 213) state: "In situations where motives, attitudes, beliefs, and values direct much, if not most of human activity, the most sophisticated instrumentation we possess is still the careful observer—the human being who can watch, see, listen . . . question, probe, and finally analyze and organize his direct experience."

CHAPTER 7

Mining Data
from Documents

In interviews and observations, the researcher gathers data for the purpose of his or her investigation. In so doing, both techniques "intrude as a foreign element into the social setting they would describe, they create as well as measure attitudes, they elicit atypical roles and responses, they are limited to those who are accessible and will cooperate" (Webb and others, 1981, p. 1). Documents, on the other hand, are usually produced for reasons other than research and therefore are not subject to the same limitations. They are, in fact, a ready-made source of data easily accessible to the imaginative and resourceful investigator. This chapter examines the nature of documents, their limitations and strengths, their various forms, and their use in case study research.

Nature of Documents

In referring to data other than those obtained through interviews or observations, the term *documents* has been chosen mainly because of the use of written materials in case study research. Holsti (1969, p. 1) defines documents "in the broad sense of any communication" and includes as examples novels, newspapers, love songs, diaries, psychiatric interviews, and the like. Goetz and LeCompte (1984, p. 153) use the term *artifact* to cover "the range of written and symbolic records kept by or on participants in a social group." Riley (1963) and Selltiz, Jahoda, Deutsch, and Cook (1959) talk about "available" materials or data. By this they mean just about anything in existence prior to the research at hand: "The researcher may make use of letters or television transcripts, historical documents or journalistic accounts, tribal artifacts or works of art. He may analyze the records of corporations, police courts, or the U.S. Bureau of the Census. He may reexamine . . . the already completed studies of other scholars. As all these and diverse other materials accumulate, it may well be that increasing numbers of researchers will find that the data they need have already been gathered" (pp. 240–241). Recently Webb and others (1981) have introduced researchers to the potential usefulness of physical evidence or traces as a source of data. Although this chapter concentrates on written documents, the general discussion applies to all forms of data not gathered through interviews or observations.

Limitations and Strengths of Documents

In judging the value of a data source, one can ask whether it contains information or insights relevant to the research question and whether it can be acquired in a reasonably practical yet systematic manner. If these two questions can be answered in the affirmative, there is no reason not to use a particular source of data. Documents or artifacts have been underused in qualitative research, however. Glaser and Strauss (1967) think that "the extremely limited range of qualitative materials used by sociologists is largely due to the focus on verification" (p. 162). They also note that researchers prefer to produce their own data, that the use of documents is too much like historical research, that they want "to see the concrete situation and informants in person," and that they distrust their own competency in using documentary materials (p. 163).

Preferences for other sources of data may reflect a researcher's uncertainty about the potential of documents for yielding knowledge and insight. But the researcher's caution may also reflect some of the limitations inherent in this data source. Several limitations stem from the basic difference between this source and data gleaned from interviews or observations—that documentary data have not been developed for research purposes. The materials may therefore be incomplete from a research perspective. In contrast to field notes, available materials may not "afford a continuity of unfolding events in the kind of detail that the theorist requires" (Glaser and Strauss, 1967, p. 182). Whether personal accounts or official documents are involved, the source may provide unrepresentative samples: "Often no one on the project keeps very good notes on processes, few memoranda are generated, and, even more often, the only writing that is done is in response to funders' requests for technical reports or other periodic statements about the progress of the program or project. If no documents exist, however, or if the documents are sparse and seem uninformative, this ought to tell the inquirer something about the context" (Guba and Lincoln, 1981, pp. 234–235).

Because documents are not produced for research purposes, the information they offer may "come to the researcher in a form he does not fully understand." Furthermore, such data "may not fit present definitions of the concepts under scrutiny; they may lack correspondence with the conceptual model" (Riley, 1963, p. 254). This is of course more of a problem when documents are used as secondary data sources to verify findings based on other data. If documents are used as part of the process of inductively building categories and theoretical constructs as in qualitative case studies, then their "fit" with preestablished concepts or models is less of a concern.

A third major problem with documentary materials is determining their authenticity and accuracy. Even public records that purport to be objective and accurate contain built-in biases that a researcher may not be aware of. For example, the incidence and frequency of crimes reported in police records may be a function of how certain crimes are defined and a particular department's procedures for reporting them. Personal documents are subject to purposeful or nonpurposeful deception. There is likely to be, for example, an underestimation of income in a personal income tax report versus an overestimation of expenses in a grant proposal. Distortion in personal documents may be unintentional in that the writer is unaware of his or her biases or simply does not remember accurately. Selltiz, Jahoda, Deutsch, and Cook (1959, p. 325) quote Augustine, who noted this problem of authenticity in his famous personal document, *Confessions:* "And when they hear me confessing of myself, how do they know whether I speak the truth?"

Determining the authenticity and accuracy of documents is part of the research process. Burgess (1982) writes that documents should not be used in isolation: It is the investigator's responsibility to determine as much as possible about the document, its origins and reasons for being written, its author, and the context in which it was written. Guba and Lincoln (1981, pp. 238–239), citing Clark (1967), list the questions one might ask about the authenticity of documents:

- What is the history of the document?
- How did it come into my hands?
- What guarantee is there that it is what it pretends to be?
- Is the document complete, as originally constructed?
- Has it been tampered with or edited?
- If the document is genuine, under what circumstances and for what purposes was it produced?
- Who was/is the author?
- What was he trying to accomplish? For whom was the document intended?
- What were the maker's sources of information? Does the document represent an eyewitness account, a secondhand account, a reconstruction of an event long prior to the writing, an interpretation?
- What was or is the maker's bias?
- To what extent was the writer likely to want to tell the truth?
- Do other documents exist that might shed addi-

tional light on the same story, event, project, program, context? If so, are they available, accessible? Who holds them?

These questions apply to historical documents as well as to anonymous project reports and sources who wish to remain anonymous such as "Deep Throat" of the 1974 Watergate case (Webb and others, 1981).

Despite these limitations, documents are a good source of data for numerous reasons. To begin with, they often meet Dexter's (1970) criteria for selecting a particular data collection strategy—that is, documents should be used when it appears they will yield *"better* data or *more* data or data *at less cost* than other tactics"* (p. 11). Many documents are easily accessible, free, and contain information that would take an investigator enormous time and effort to gather on his or her own.

Furthermore, documents may be the *only* means of studying certain problems. Riley (1963) notes four areas where documents are crucial to an investigation: (1) historical studies in which events can no longer be observed and informants may not recall or be available for recall; (2) cross-cultural studies where settings are remote or inaccessible; (3) studies that rely on technical expertise such as a doctor's report; and (4) studies of intimate personal relationships that cannot be observed and which people are often reluctant to discuss.

The data found in documents can be used in the same manner as data from interviews or observations. The data can furnish descriptive information, verify emerging hypotheses, advance new categories and hypotheses, offer historical understanding, track change and development, and so on. Glaser and Strauss (1967, p. 179) point to the usefulness of documents for theory building—a process that "begs for comparative analysis. The library offers a *fantastic range* of comparison groups, if only the researcher has the ingenuity to discover them."

One of the greatest advantages in using documentary material is its stability. Unlike interviewing and observation, the investigator does not alter what is being studied by his or her presence. Documentary data are "objective" sources of data compared to other forms. Such data have also been called "un-obtrusive." Webb and others' (1966) classic book on unobtrusive measures in its revised form is titled *Nonreactive Measures in the Social Sciences* (1981) because, they write, "we came to realize over the years that the original title was not the best one since it was the nonreactivity of the measures rather than their unobtrusiveness that was of major concern" (p. ix). Nonreactive measures include physical traces, official records, private documents, and simple and contrived observations.

Finally, documentary data are particularly good sources for *qualitative* case studies because they can ground an investigation in the context of the problem being investigated. Analysis of this data source "lends contextual richness and helps to ground an inquiry in the milieu of the writer. This grounding in real-world issues and day-to-day concerns is ultimately what the naturalistic inquiry is working toward" (Guba and Lincoln, 1981, p. 234).

Thus, like any other source of data, documents have their limitations and their advantages. Because they are produced for reasons other than research, they may be fragmentary, they may not fit the conceptual framework of the research, and their authenticity may be difficult to determine. On the other hand, because they exist independent of a research agenda, they are non-reactive—that is, unaffected by the research process. They are a product of the context in which they were produced and therefore grounded in the real world. Finally, many documents or artifacts cost little or nothing and are often easy to obtain.

Types of Documents

As noted earlier, the term *document* in this discussion refers to a wide range of written and physical material. Public or archival records, personal documents, and physical traces are three major types of documents available to the researcher for analysis. Moreover, a researcher can create documents for the purpose of the investigation.

Public records are "the ongoing, continuing records of a society" (Webb and others, 1981, p. 78). They include actuarial records of births, deaths, and marriages; the U.S. census; police records and court transcripts; agency records; program documents; mass media; government documents; and so on. Locating public records is limited only by one's imagination and industriousness. As Guba and Lincoln (1981, p. 253) note: "The first and most important injunction to anyone looking for official records is to presume that if an event happened, some record of it exists."

For those interested in educational questions, there are numerous sources of public documents—discussions of educational issues and bills in the *Congressional Record*, federal, state, and private agency reports, individual program records, the statistical data base of the Center for Educational Statistics (CES). Since many case studies are at the program level, it is particularly important to seek out the paper trail for what it can reveal about the program—"things that cannot be observed because they may have taken place before the evaluation began, because they include private interchanges to which the educator is not directly privy, and because they reflect aspects of the organization that may be idealized" (Patton, 1980, p. 152). Ideally this paper trail includes "all routine records on clients, all correspondence from and to program staff, financial and budget records, organizational rules, regulations, memoranda, charts, and any other official or unofficial documents generated by or for the program" (Patton, 1980, p. 152). Such documents not only provide valuable information about the program itself, but they can also stimulate thinking "about important questions to pursue through more direct observations and interviewing" (p. 152).

Another source of information easily accessible but often overlooked is previous studies. In this situation the researcher has to rely on someone else's description and interpretation of data rather than having the raw data as a basis for analysis. For large-scale or cross-cultural research, relying on previous studies may be the only realistic way to conduct the investigation. An example of this data source would be the Human Relations Area File (Murdock, 1983; Murdock and others, 1982). This file is a compilation of ethnographic studies of more than 350 societies. Data are classified and coded by cultural group and also by more than 700 topics. Education is one broad topic under which one can find subtopics such as elementary education, educational theory and methods, students, vocational education, and so on. The index is organized so that a researcher can investigate the educational practices of one cultural group or a specific educational topic such as "student uprisings" across many cultures.

"Every literate society," writes Kidder (1981b, p. 286), "produces a variety of material intended to inform, entertain, or persuade the populace." Popular media forms such as television, films, radio, newspapers, literary works, photography, cartoons, and the like are another source of "public" data. Mass communication materials are especially good sources for dealing with questions about some aspect of society at a given time, for comparing groups on a certain dimension, or for tracking cultural change and trends. They "concentrate on what is of current interest, and that concentration makes it possible to track many phenomena and index the growth and decline of public interest in them" (Webb and others, 1981, p. 120). Studies have been conducted, for example, on the roles of blacks in television, the presence of ageism in cartoons, and teenage culture in movies.

In contrast to public sources of data, personal documents refer to *"individuals' written first-person accounts of the whole or parts of their lives or their reflections on a specific event or topic"* (Taylor and Bogdan, 1984, p. 113). Such documents include diaries, letters, home videos, sermons, children's growth records, scrapbooks and photo albums, calendars, autobiographies, and travel logs. Selltiz, Jahoda, Deutsch, and Cook (1959) note that "the rationale for the use of personal documents is similar to that for the use of observational techniques. What the latter may achieve for overt behavior, the former can do for inner experiences: to reveal to the social scientist life as it is lived without the interference of research" (p. 325). Such documents can tell the researcher about the inner meaning of everyday events, or they may yield descriptions of "rare and extraordinary events in human life" (p. 327) such as can be found in Admiral Byrd's report of his experiences alone at the South Pole or Helen Keller's account of overcoming extraordinary physical handicaps.

Personal documents are a reliable source of data concerning a person's attitudes, beliefs, and view of the world. But because they are *personal* documents, the material is highly subjective—"the writer himself and alone selects the facts, incidents, and events which are to him most important" (Burnett, 1977, p. 10). Obviously, these documents are not representative or necessarily reliable accounts of what occurred. Burgess (1982, p. 132) summarizes the nature of personal documents:

> The field researcher needs to consider: Is the material trustworthy? Is the material atypical? Has the material been edited and refined? Does the autobiographical material only contain highlights of life that are considered interesting? Furthermore, it could be argued that the material is automatically biased as only certain people produce autobiographies and keep diaries; there is self-selectivity involved in the sample of material available; they do not provide a complete historical record. Nevertheless, such material does provide a subjective account of the situation it records; it is a reconstruction of part of life. Furthermore, it provides an account that is based on the author's experience.

A third type of document, broadly defined, is what has come to be known as *physical trace material.* Physical traces are defined as "any changes in the physical environment due to human actions" (Rathje, 1979, pp. 75–76). Examples of physical evidence being used in research studies are provided by Webb and others (1981, p. 2):

• One investigator wanted to know the relationship between reported and actual beer consumption. He obtained a "front door" measure by asking residents of houses how much beer they consumed each week and a "back door" measure by counting the beer cans in their garbage cans. The back door measure resulted in a considerably higher estimate of beer consumption.

- The degree of fear induced by a ghost-story-telling session can be measured by noting the shrinking diameter of a circle of seated children.
- Library withdrawals have been used to demonstrate the effect of the introduction of television into a community. Fiction titles dropped but nonfiction titles were unaffected.
- A child's interest in Christmas can be demonstrated by distortions in the size of Santa Claus drawings.

There are two basic means of studying physical traces—by noting their erosion, which is the degree of wear, and by noting their accretion, which is the degree of accumulation. The wear and tear on floor tiles in front of a museum exhibit as a sign of public interest is a well-known example of erosion (Webb and others, 1966); the accumulation of beer cans in the preceding list is a good example of accretion.

Because physical traces can usually be measured, they are most often suited for obtaining information on incidence and frequency of behavior. They are also a good check on information obtained from interviews or surveys. In case study research, most physical trace measures are used to supplement data gathered through interviews and observations. One might, for example, compare the wear and tear on computer terminals in a school program that purports to include computer literacy in its basic curriculum. Other advantages of using trace measures are noted by Rathje (1979, pp. 78–79):

- trace measures record the results of actual behavior, not reported or experimental approximations;
- trace measures are usually *nonreactive* and *unobtrusive*. Since they are applied after behavior has occurred they do not modify the behavior they seek to study;
- material traces are ubiquitous and readily available for study;
- because material traces are applied to inanimate

objects, they usually require minimal coopera-
tion and inconvenience from human subjects;

- because the number of measures of traces depends upon the recorder's interest rather than
informant patience, a variety of interrelated behaviors can often be studied at once;

- because of the minimal inconvenience and ex-
pense to informants, trace measures can be used
over long time periods as longitudinal monitoring devices.

A fourth type of document that is likely to find its way
into a case study investigation is a document prepared by the
researcher for the specific purpose of learning more about the
situation, person, or event being investigated. The researcher
might request that someone keep a diary or log of activities during the course of the investigation. Or a life history of an individual or historical account of a program might be solicited to
illuminate the present situation. A researcher's photographs are
another example of this type of document. Such photographs,
often taken in conjunction with participant observation, provide a "means of remembering and studying detail that might
be overlooked if a photographic image were not available for re-
flection" (Bogdan and Biklen, 1982, p. 108).

Quantitative data produced by the investigator also fall
into this category of documents. Projective tests, attitudinal
measures, content examinations, statistical data from surveys on
any number of topics—all can be treated as documents in support of a case study investigation. In a case study of a county
health workers' training program, for example, data were collected from written questionnaires as well as through observation and interviews. Results of the survey became supporting
documentary material for the observation and interview-based
findings of the study (Dominick and Cervero, 1987).

In summary, then, documents comprise a broad range of
materials available to the researcher who is creative in seeking
them out. Literally millions of public and private documents as
well as physical traces of human behavior can be used as primary or secondary sources of data. In the final section of this

chapter, the process of using documents for research purposes is examined.

Using Documents in Case Study Research

Using documentary material as data is not much different from using interviews or observations. Glaser and Strauss (1967) compare fieldwork with library research: "When someone stands in the library stacks, he is, metaphorically, surrounded by voices begging to be heard. Every book, every magazine article, represents at least one person who is equivalent to the anthropologist's informant or the sociologist's interviewee. In those publications, people converse, announce positions, argue with a range of eloquence, and describe events or scenes in ways entirely comparable to what is seen and heard during fieldwork" (p. 163). Whether in fieldwork or library work, the data collection is guided by educated hunches and tentative hypotheses. Although the search is systematic, both settings also allow for the accidental uncovering of valuable data. Tracking down leads, being open to new insights, and being sensitive to the data are the same whether one is interviewing, observing, or analyzing documents. Since the investigator is the primary instrument for gathering data, he or she relies on skills and intuition to find and interpret data from documents.

Finding relevant materials is the first step in the process. As mentioned, this is generally a systematic procedure that evolves from the topic of inquiry itself. A case study of a back-to-industry program for postsecondary faculty logically led the researcher to memos, background papers, advertising material, application forms, and final reports on the project (Kline, 1981). A case study of an individual's project on learning to build a greenhouse might lead to examining notes on the project, pamphlets or books gathered by the person telling how to do it, the finished product itself, and so on. Other discoveries happen serendipitously. The logical places to look are libraries, historical societies, archives, and institutional files. Others have located personal documents like letters and diaries by placing advertisements in newspapers and newsletters (Taylor and Bogdan, 1984).

Selltiz, Jahoda, Deutsch, and Cook (1959) observe that

finding pertinent documents hinges to some extent on the investigator's ability to think creatively about the problem under study: "The use of such data demands *a capacity to ask many different questions related to the research problem.* By definition, the purpose for which available records have been collected is different from the purpose for which the social scientist wishes to use them" (p. 318). Thus the researcher must keep an open mind when it comes to discovering useful documents.

Once documents have been located, their authenticity must be assessed. Since they were not produced for the researcher, the investigator must try to "reconstruct the process by which the data were originally assembled by somebody else" (Riley, 1963, p. 252). It is important to determine "the conditions under which these data were produced, what specific methodological and technical decisions may have been made, ... and the consequent impact on the nature of the data now to be taken over" (p. 252). In evaluating artifacts—that is, objects used or produced by a particular cultural group—Goetz and LeCompte (1984) suggest that the researcher ask such questions as: What is the history of its production and use? How is its use allocated? Is its selection biased? How might it be distorted or falsified?

After assessing the authenticity and nature of documents or artifacts, the researcher must adopt some system for coding and cataloging them. If at all possible, written documents should be copied and artifacts "photographed, filmed, or taped" (Goetz and LeCompte, 1984, p. 155). By establishing basic descriptive categories early on for coding, the researcher will have easy access to information in the analysis and interpretation stage. An application to a specific career enhancement award program, for example, could be filed by the applicant's type of employment, dollar amount of request, sex, geographic location, or nature of the project proposed.

In qualitative case studies, a form of content analysis is used to analyze documents. Essentially content analysis is a systematic procedure for describing the content of communications. Historians and literary critics have long used content analysis to analyze historical documents and literary works. Modern content analysis has most often been applied to communications media (newspapers, periodicals, television, film) and has had a strong quantitative focus. A major concern has been measuring the frequency and variety of messages and confirming hypotheses. Most research designs using content analysis are sequential in nature—"moving from category construction to sampling, data collection, data analysis and interpretation" (Altheide, 1987, p. 68). Data collection and coding are often carried out by novices using protocols and trained to count units of analysis.

Quantification need not be a component of content analysis, however. One can also assess the *character* of the data (Selltiz, Jahoda, Deutsch, and Cook, 1959, p. 336). Altheide (1987) describes how qualitative content analysis differs from conventional content analysis: "Ethnographic content analysis is used to document and understand the communication of meaning, as well as to verify theoretical relationships. Its distinctive characteristic is the reflexive and highly interactive nature of the investigator, concepts, data collection and analysis. . . . The investigator is continually central, although protocols may be used in later phases of the research. . . . The aim is to be systematic and analytic, but not rigid. Although categories and 'variables' initially guide the study, others are allowed and expected to emerge throughout the study" (p. 68). Essentially, qualitative content analysis looks for insights in which "situations, settings, styles, images, meanings and nuances are key topics" (Altheide, 1987, p. 68). The process involves the simultaneous coding of raw data and constructing categories that capture relevant characteristics of the document's content. A detailed discussion of inductive data analysis can be found in the next chapter.

Summary

Documents—broadly defined to include public records, personal papers, physical traces, and artifacts—are a third major source of data in case study research. Although some documents might be prepared at the investigator's request (such as a respondent keeping a diary or writing a life history), most are produced independent of the research study. They are thus non-reactive and grounded in the context under study. Because they are produced for reasons other than the study at hand, some ingenuity is needed in locating documents that bear on the problem and then in analyzing their content. Congruency between documents and the research problem depends on the researcher's flexibility in construing the problem and related questions. Such a stance is particularly fitting in qualitative case studies which, by their very nature, are emergent in design and inductive in analysis. Documents of all types can help the researcher uncover meaning, develop understanding, and discover insights relevant to the research problem.

PART THREE

ANALYZING
AND REPORTING
CASE STUDY DATA

Choosing a *qualitative* case study research design presupposes a certain view of the world that in turn defines how one selects a sample, collects data, analyzes them, and approaches issues of validity, reliability, and ethics. Part Three consists of four chapters that address the later stages of the research process, including two chapters on analyzing qualitative data, one chapter on producing valid and reliable knowledge in an ethical manner, and one chapter on writing the case study report.

Having separate chapters on data analysis and issues of validity, reliability, and ethics may be somewhat misleading to the reader in that qualitative research is not a linear, step-by-step process. Data collection and analysis is a *simultaneous* activity in qualitative research. Analysis begins with the first interview, the first observation, the first document read. Emerging insights, hunches, and tentative hypotheses direct the next phase of data collection, which in turn leads to refinement or reformulation of one's questions, and so on. It is an interactive process throughout which the investigator is concerned with producing believable and trustworthy findings. Unlike experimental designs where validity and reliability are accounted for before the investigation, rigor in a qualitative case study derives from the researcher's presence, the nature of the interaction between researcher and participants, the triangulation of data, the interpretation of perceptions, and rich, thick description.

It follows, then, that the final report of a qualitative study will look different from the final report of a conventional research design. In comparing the rhetoric of a quantitative study and a qualitative study of the same problem, Firestone (1987, p. 19) notes that different strategies are used to persuade the reader of the authenticity of the findings: "The quantitative study must convince the reader that procedures have been followed faithfully because very little concrete description of what anyone does is provided. The qualitative study provides the reader with a depiction in enough detail to show that the author's conclusion 'makes sense.' " The qualitative study reviewed by Firestone included "telling quotes from interviews, a description of agency staffing patterns, and excerpts from agency history. . . . The details are convincing," he writes, "because they create a gestalt that makes sense to the reader" (p. 19).

To further illustrate the totality of the qualitative research process, consider Elbaz's (1981, 1983) qualitative case study of a teacher—in particular, a study of the teacher's practical knowledge. A qualitative case study design was selected, she writes, "because vivid and full description of a single case is not only educationally valuable in itself but also particularly called for in the present state of our understanding of teachers' knowledge." The case study was seen "as a method well suited to attain an understanding of the teacher's knowledge from her own point of view, and thus to exemplify and embody the conception of practical knowledge" (1981, p. 51). Elbaz goes on to explain why a particular teacher was chosen to be interviewed for the study: "One guarantee of capturing the teacher's knowledge in a real way was the choice of a teacher who was committed to her work, able to articulate her point of view, and interested in doing so. . . . The teacher's awareness of and ability to articulate her knowledge, which might be seen as a barrier to getting at the 'facts' in an experimentally oriented study, are here precisely the matters I wished to observe and document through the interview situation" (p. 51).

Elbaz grapples with the notions of validity and reliability and discusses them in conjunction with the way data are gathered and analyzed. The research was guided, she writes, by "the view that the research subject is a person, who has feelings, values, needs, and purposes which condition his or her participation in the research. This assumption was the basis for the decision to disclose my purposes and interpretations to the teacher and to invite her participation in the interpretive process" (1981, p. 51). Of analyzing and presenting the data, Elbaz writes: "Because the categories used in the final analysis developed in response to the data, the study moved toward the goal of accounting for the teacher's practical knowledge from a teacher's perspective. The analytic tools used were, of course, mine, not the teacher's, but these tools were shaped by the effort to regard the teacher as a person, to become aware of the reality of her work situation as she encountered it, and to give an account that was consistent with (though not identical to) her view of her work" (p. 51).

In the last four chapters of this book, readers will get a sense of the *interactive* nature of data collection, analysis, and reporting. Data analysis in qualitative research very much depends on the investigator's sensitivity and analytic skills. Whether one is analyzing data in a single case study or across several individual cases, the process is inductive. In both a single case study and cross-case studies, data are sifted through, combined, reduced, interpreted. In so doing, the uniqueness of a particular quote, the subtlety of a particular observation, may be obscured. Throughout the analysis and reporting phases of qualitative research there is a tension between "descriptive excess" (Lofland, 1971, p. 129) and coming up with "reasonable conclusions and generalizations based on a preponderance of the data" (Taylor and Bogdan, 1984, p. 139). This tension extends to issues of validity and reliability—for the more grounded in supporting detail one's findings are, the more credible and trustworthy they are. The chapters in this part of the book are presented with the awareness that detailed instructions in analyzing and reporting qualitative case study data, though helpful, are merely guidelines in need of interpretation and application by the single most important component in qualitative research: the investigator.

CHAPTER 8

The Components
of Data Analysis

Preceding chapters have explained how to gather data for a case study through interviews, observations, and documents. This chapter concentrates on how to analyze the data once they have been collected. Devoting a separate chapter to data analysis is misleading, however, since collection and analysis should be a simultaneous process in qualitative research. It is, in fact, the timing of analysis and the integration of analysis with other tasks that distinguish a qualitative design from traditional positivistic research (Goetz and LeCompte, 1984). A qualitative design is emergent: One does not know whom to interview, what to ask, or where to look next without analyzing data as they are collected. Hunches, working hypotheses, and educated guesses direct the investigator's attention to certain data and then to refining and/or verifying one's hunches. The process of data collection and analysis is recursive and dynamic. But this is not to say that the analysis is finished when all the data have been collected. Quite the opposite. Analysis becomes more intensive once all the data are in, even though analysis has been an ongoing activity. In this chapter we examine the several dimensions of data analysis—including analysis during data collection, the devising of categories, and the building of theory.

Analysis During Data Collection

At the outset of a qualitative case study, the investigator knows what the problem is and has defined the case that will be studied in order to address the problem. But the researcher does not know what will be discovered, what or whom to concentrate on, or what the final analysis will be like. The final product of a case study is shaped by the data that are collected and the analysis that accompanies the entire process. Without ongoing analysis one runs the risk of ending up with data that are unfocused, repetitious, and overwhelming in the sheer volume of material that needs to be processed. Data that have been analyzed while being collected are both parsimonious and illuminating. Bogdan and Biklen (1982) offer nine helpful suggestions for analyzing data as they are being collected:

1. Force yourself to make decisions that narrow the study. "You must discipline yourself not to pursue everything . . . or else you are likely to wind up with data too diffuse and inappropriate for what you decide to do. The more data you have on a given topic, setting, or subjects, the easier it will be to think deeply about it and the more productive you are likely to be when you attempt the final analysis" (p. 147).
2. Force yourself to make decisions concerning the type of study you want to conduct. "You should try to make clear in your own mind, for example, whether you want to do a full description of a setting or whether you are interested in generating theory about a particular aspect of it" (p. 147).
3. Develop analytic questions. "Some researchers bring general questions to a study. These are important because they give focus to data collection and help organize it as you proceed. . . . We suggest that shortly after you enter the field, you assess which questions you brought with you are relevant and which ones should be reformulated to direct your work" (p. 147).
4. Plan data collection sessions according to what you find in previous observations. "In light of what you find when you

periodically review your fieldnotes, plan to pursue specific leads in your next data collection session" (p. 149).

5. Write many "observer's comments" as you go. "The idea is to stimulate critical thinking about what you see and to become more than a recording machine" (p. 149).

6. Write memos to yourself about what you are learning. "These memos can provide a time to reflect on issues raised in the setting and how they relate to larger theoretical, methodological, and substantive issues" (p. 149).

7. Try out ideas and themes on subjects. "While not everyone should be asked, and while not all you hear may be helpful, key informants, under the appropriate circumstances, can help advance your analysis, especially to fill in the holes of description" (p. 153).

8. Begin exploring literature while you are in the field. "We believe that after you have been in the field for a while, going through the substantive literature in the area you are studying will enhance analysis" (p. 153).

9. Play with metaphors, analogies, and concepts. "Nearsightedness plagues most research. . . . Ask the question, 'What does this remind me of?' " (p. 153). "Another way to expand analytic horizons is to try to raise concrete relations and happenings observed in a particular setting to a higher level of abstraction" (p. 154).

Data collection and analysis is indeed an ongoing process that can extend indefinitely. There is almost always another person who could be interviewed, another observation that could be conducted, always more documents to be reviewed. When should the researcher stop this phase of the investigation and begin intensive data analysis? The answer depends on some very practical concerns, such as depleting the time and money allocated to the project or running out of mental energy. Lincoln and Guba (1985) list four theoretical guidelines for ending the data collection phase of a study:

> *Exhaustion of sources* (although sources may be recycled and tapped multiple times); *saturation of*

> *categories* (continuing data collection produces tiny
> increments of new information in comparison to
> the effort expended to get them); *emergence of*
> *regularities*—the sense of "integration" (although
> care must be exercised to avoid a false conclusion
> occasioned by regularities occurring at a more sim-
> plistic level than the inquirer should accept); and
> *over-extension*—the sense that new information
> being unearthed is very far removed from the core
> of any of the viable categories that have emerged
> (and does not contribute usefully to the emergence
> of additional viable categories) [p. 350].

Once a decision has been made to end simultaneous data
collection and analysis, the information must be organized so
that intensive analysis can begin. All the information one has
about the case should be brought together—interview logs or
transcripts, field notes, reports, records, the investigator's own
documents, physical traces, and reflective memos. All this material needs to be organized in some fashion so that data are easily
retrievable. Yin (1984) calls this organized material the *case
study data base,* which he differentiates from the case study report. In a similar fashion, Patton (1980) differentiates the *case
record* from the final case study: "The case record pulls together and organizes the voluminous case data into a comprehensive
primary resource package. The case record includes all the major information that will be used in doing the case analysis and
case study. Information is edited, redundancies are sorted out,
parts are fitted together, and the case record is organized for
ready access either chronologically [or] topically. The case record must be complete but manageable" (p. 313).

Developing the case record involves some fairly simple
sorting of all the data. The goal is to be able to locate specific
data during intensive analysis. The data therefore need to be organized according to some scheme that makes sense to the investigator and then indexed accordingly. A case record of a
bank's training program, for example, might organize the data
according to the various training components, employees in-

volved in the training, dates when observations and interviews were conducted, and so on.

Intensive Analysis

Several levels of analysis and interpretation are possible in case study research. Indeed, some case studies are little more than case records—basically descriptive accounts of the phenomenon under study that contain little analysis or interpretation of the data. The material may even be presented according to the categories used to organize the raw data. What makes them case studies is the narrative structure used to present the data. Lightfoot's award-winning study (1983) of good high schools presents descriptive portraits of six successful high schools. She says of her case descriptions:

> Not only did I want to honor these schools, applaud their efforts and acclaim their successes; I also recognized that it was important for readers to be able to place these high schools in context—visualize the terrain, the community, the neighborhood streets, and the people. As a form that is partly shaped by aesthetic considerations, portraiture is to some extent a visual medium, full of powerful imagery. If I were to mask details of context or provide misleading descriptors, for example, I would begin to compromise the portrait [p. 22].

In another study, Houle (1984) investigated patterns of inquiry used by lifelong learners throughout history. He presents each case as a descriptive study. As in Lightfoot's book, each description can stand alone. Both researchers do include a concluding chapter that offers generalizations drawn from all the cases. Exhibit 4 presents excerpts from one of Houle's case studies exploring oratory as a basic teaching method. Note how the rich, thick description transports the reader to the event.

Data analysis is the process of making sense out of one's data. Even in the examples of Lightfoot and Houle, data have

Exhibit 4. Example of a Descriptive Case Study.

If you entered the great hall of McCormick Place in Chicago on a June evening in 1971, you were immediately confronted by a long row of tables at which books and phonograph records were for sale, with, for example, a $4.95 authorized biography of Graham going at the special rate of $2.50. Beyond those tables were 38,000 seats, but your choice among them was limited. Some were held for those with "blue and white tickets," whatever that might mean. Some were set aside for groups. Some were reserved for counselors, ushers, and the press. Most of the seats near the door were kept for latecomers. Men with bull-horns were needed to direct the general flow of traffic, but for the most part in-comers were gently urged in one direction by ushers and prevented from going in other directions by barriers. Eventually you came to the place where you could exercise a choice but it was not a wide one. Every seat must be taken, and people were held shoulder to shoulder by linked chairs. When one section was full, another was opened. There must be close, direct, human contact of a physical sort. . . .

The ushers are indispensable to the entire process. They range from perhaps twenty-five to seventy-five years of age; they are neatly dressed with carefully folded handkerchiefs in their breast pockets; they have fresh haircuts; and they have been either born to their calling or conditioned by years of service on Sunday mornings. Each has four to six rows of seats under his care and sees himself as the kindly shepherd of the people sitting in them. Authority rises above these first-line men in an orderly hierarchy; there are aisle captains and section captains and presumably a floor captain. These men are constantly busy; once the need to seat their flock has been met, they confer with one another endlessly, answer questions from the audience, volunteer information about the evening's program, and, if need be, care for distress or disturbance.

The setting itself is in no sense dramatic, only big. No bold design catches the eye, no banners wave, no striking symbols are to be seen. Later on, there will be no sudden darkenings of the room or the stadium, no beams of light picking out an isolated figure in the darkness, no use of projected images, no hidden electric fans causing banners to wave. No orchestra will play; the only music will be provided by piano or organ. None of the devices of modern industrial design or of the packaging of performance are visible.

The evocation is of something far different and far more familiar. The meeting place feels comfortable to its audiences because it has been made to look as much as possible like customary places of lower- and middle-class pomp and ceremony: the Protestant church, the high school auditorium, or the converted gymnasium or movie theater that is being used for graduation exercises. The people present know where they are because they have been there so often. Only the scale has changed. In Chicago, a banner stretching across the background of the rostrum said: "Jesus said, 'I am the way, the truth, and the life.' John 14:6"; it was fifty feet long. The chorus was made up not of twenty or a hundred voices but of two thousand. The platform was very large. The piano and organ were electri-

Exhibit 4. Example of a Descriptive Case Study, Cont'd.

cally amplified, so that 38,000 people could hear every note. The runway that projected forward from the platform was edged with the familiar shapes of ferns and ornamental trees. At the base of the lectern was an arrangement of flowers like those at christenings, weddings, and funerals—but incomparably larger. The hall itself was brilliantly lighted throughout, but, in addition, three massed rows of spotlights focused on the platform. . . .

A strong sense of community pervades the hall. It is felt most deeply by the members of a local church congregation who know one another, come from the same community, have planned and undertaken the trip, sit together, and will go home in the same bus. As the service proceeds, the feeling of togetherness spreads to the entire assemblage. We have so much in common. We heard the choir rehearsing before the service. We focused our cameras on the young man who stood silently at the lectern for a half hour before the service; when Billy comes out we are sure to get good photographs. Isn't it wonderful how many people are pouring in? We applaud during the program whenever the success of the Crusade is mentioned. We sing familiar songs. We rise and sit down as directed. We look up passages in the Bibles we have brought. We laugh comfortably at the witticisms. We catch our breaths with astonishment when a celebrity is introduced. We make our financial contributions willingly, eager to help the great Crusade go on. We speak to one another approvingly of the number of young people present this evening. When a speaker makes a telling point, we say "amen." We talk about past Crusades and hope for future ones. We exchange gossip about Billy and the members of his team. We nudge our children and remind them that this is a night they will remember all their lives. We make plans to see all future telecasts, especially the one of tonight's program. We say over and over again how nice it is that Billy has had a chance to come back to Chicago-land, which means so much to him; other people may claim him but he is really one of ours, having gone to one of our colleges and having had his first pastorate here. . . .

The pace quickens. With no introduction, Graham bounds to the lectern at the front end of the long runway. He welcomes the group, gives thanks to various people, tells the audience how close Chicago "and the tri-state area" are to his own heart, makes a little witticism, and describes in detail what will be happening each subsequent evening during the Crusade. He is succeeded by several events: Barrows recommending a magazine, a hymn by the choir, another solo by another artist, Barrows recommending a book, a hymn by the choir and audience, and then an introduction of the second most important event of the evening. It is a talk by someone who has found God, often by listening to Graham. The speaker may be a big league baseball player, a handicapped person in a wheelchair, a former member of a youth gang or of the White House staff, or a leader of the advertising profession. This speech is brief, well-rehearsed, and movingly spoken. Then another song by soloist and choir. Then comes the main event of the evening.

(continued on next page)

Exhibit 4. Example of a Descriptive Case Study, Cont'd.

The man who is the focal point of this elaborate setting and process is taller than his co-workers, erect, and with a springing step. His face is exactly like the one shown in his newspaper photographs except, of course, that it is not black and white but ruddy. His hair sweeps back to a moderate length, its smooth perfection sometimes set off by a little duck tail. His face is lean and his build athletic.

His countenance is mobile, although he never smiles. He uses his hands with extraordinary effectiveness and swiftness and has a large repertoire of gestures, each distinct but flowing into one another with smooth perfection. The right-hand index finger is pointed toward the audience or toward heaven. He clenches one or both fists, or his hands rapidly revolve around one another. A characteristic gesture is made with either hand. It is a swift vertical movement, followed by a swift horizontal one. "He sent his son" (vertical movement) "to die for you" (horizontal movement). The symbolism of the cross must be evident to many and subliminal to others. A frequent mannerism is to thrust his head forward from his body with the chin stretched out as far as possible and the lips tightly pressed. It is a defiant look that says, "I have said something you must hear; if you don't, it is at your cost." His most celebrated posture comes at the end, while he is waiting for people to come forward. Then he stands erect except for a bowed head, his eyes closed, his upper lip resting on his clasped hands.

His voice is vibrant and alive. He knows, as does any orator, that it lies at the heart of his success. While sitting on the platform, he sprays his throat surreptitiously with a hand atomizer, and he takes a sudden last sip of water before he goes forward to preach. His voice has been thoroughly trained, and he uses it to the full limit of its not extraordinary range. His accent is American of the middle-South variety, particularly noticeable in his final "r's" and "o's"; he says "fathuh" and "heah" and "tomorruh." He thunders and he speaks softly and sometimes does one immediately following the other. He can be the great spellbinder, his blue eyes flashing fire. He can speak confidentially. He can be mildly humorous, although only rarely. And yet, although anybody who has ever taken a course in public speaking would realize that Graham is using his voice with great art, he never seems conscious of doing so. The days of the acquisition of mastery are far behind him.

Source: Houle (1984, pp. 79–86). Reprinted with permission.

been compressed and linked together in a narrative that makes sense to the reader. In the process of analysis, data are consolidated, reduced, and, to some extent, interpreted. The goal of data analysis, according to Taylor and Bogdan (1984, p. 139), is "to come up with reasonable conclusions and generalizations based on a preponderance of the data." The amount of interpretation one strives for depends on the purpose of the study as well as the end product desired. Some think that narrative description is enough. Others, such as Goetz and LeCompte (1984, p. 196), believe that ethnographers who "fail to transcend what has been termed the 'merely descriptive' . . . fail to do justice to their data. By leaving readers to draw their own conclusions, researchers risk misinterpretation. Their results also may be trivialized by readers who are unable to make connections implied, but not made explicit, by the researcher." The rest of this chapter is devoted to explaining how to analyze data in order to transcend the "merely descriptive."

Goetz and LeCompte (1984, p. 190) suggest that one begin analysis by reviewing the research proposal. Even though the investigation "may have wandered far from the original question," those questions shaped the inquiry and must be addressed in the final report. Furthermore, the proposal reminds the researcher of the "audiences for whom the study originally was intended," which is helpful information when it comes to deciding the level of analysis and format of the final report.

Next, all the data that have been gathered together and organized topically or chronologically (the case data base or the case record) should be read through several times from beginning to end. While reading, the investigator jots down notes, comments, observations, queries, in the margins. At this stage the researcher is virtually holding a conversation with the data, asking questions of it, making comments, and so on. "The notes serve to isolate the initially most striking, if not ultimately most important, aspects of the data" (Goetz and LeCompte, 1984, p. 191). One might also keep a separate running list of major ideas that cut across much of the data. "The notes taken while scanning constitute the beginning stages of organizing, abstracting, integrating, and synthesizing, which ultimately permit investigators to tell others what they have seen. The notes are developed into a primitive outline or system of classifications into which data are sorted initially. The outline begins with a search for regularities—things that happen frequently with groups of people. Patterns and regularities then are transformed into categories into which subsequent items are sorted. These categories or patterns are discovered from the data" (Goetz and LeCompte, 1984, p. 191).

At this beginning stage of analysis, Lincoln and Guba (1985, p. 344) suggest unitizing the data—identifying *"units* of information that will, sooner or later, serve as the basis for defining categories." Units come from interview transcripts, observation notes, or documents. A unit can be a phrase, a sentence, a paragraph. According to Lincoln and Guba, a unit must meet two criteria. First, it should be heuristic—that is, the unit should reveal information relevant to the study and stimulate the reader to think beyond the particular bit of information. Second, the unit should be "the smallest piece of information about something that can stand by itself—that is, it must be interpretable in the absence of any additional information other than a broad understanding of the context in which the inquiry is carried out" (p. 345).

Each unit of information can be put onto a separate index card and coded according to any number of categories ranging from situational factors (who, what, when, where) to categories representing emerging themes or concepts. A recent technique for coding and sorting data is to use a computer program designed for this purpose. A third procedure is to code the units in the margins of the interview transcripts, field notes, or documents. Photocopies can be made of the pages for later analysis of the data.

For a simple but vivid example of how to take raw data and sort them into categories, consider the task of sorting two hundred food items found in a grocery store. By comparing one item with another, you could classify the two hundred items into any number of categories. Starting with a box of cereal, for example, you could ask whether the next item, an orange, is like the first. Obviously not. There are now two piles into which the next item may or may not be placed. By this process you can sort all the items into categories of your choice. One scheme may separate the items into fresh, frozen, canned, or packaged goods. Or you could divide them by color, weight, or price. More likely, you would divide the items into common grocery store categories: meat, dairy, produce, canned goods, and so on.

These categories would be fairly comprehensive classes, each of which could be further subdivided. Produce, for example, includes fruits and vegetables. Fruits include citrus and noncitrus, domestic and exotic. All these schemes emerge logically from the "data"—that is, the food items.

Developing Categories

In addition to coding units of data by obvious factors such as who, what, when, and where, analysis involves the development of conceptual categories, typologies, or theories that interpret the data for the reader. In contrast to the simple categories used to organize the case study data base or case record, "higher level, overriding and integrating, conceptualizations—and the properties that elaborate them—tend to come later during the joint collection, coding and analysis of data" (Glaser and Strauss, 1967, p. 36). These categories are "concepts indicated by the data (and not the data itself). . . . In short, conceptual categories and properties have a life apart from the evidence that gave rise to them" (p. 36). Devising categories is largely an intuitive process, but it is also systematic and informed by the study's purpose, the investigator's orientation and knowledge, and "the constructs made explicit by the participants of the study" (Goetz and LeCompte, 1984, p. 191).

Developing categories, typologies, or themes involves looking for recurring regularities in the data. Which units of information go with each other? It is a task of comparing one unit of information with the next, as described in the grocery item example. Lincoln and Guba (1985) explain how this comparative technique can be used with their index card system:

1. Given the pile of cards that has resulted from the unitizing process, and that will be more or less haphazardly arranged, select the first card from the pile, read it, and note its contents. This first card represents the first entry in the first yet-to-be-named category. Place it to one side.

2. Select the second card, read it, and note its contents. Make a determination on tacit or intuitive grounds whether this second card is a "look-alike" or "feel-alike" with Card 1, that is, whether its contents are "essentially" similar. If so, place the second card with the first and proceed to the third card; if not, the second card represents the first entry in the second yet-to-be-named category.

3. Continue on with successive cards. For each card decide whether it is a "look/feel-alike" of cards that have already been placed in some provisional category or whether it represents a new category. Proceed accordingly.

4. After some cards have been processed the analyst may feel that a new card neither fits any of the provisionally established categories nor seems to form a new category. Other cards may now also be recognized as possibly irrelevant to the developing set. These cards should be placed into a miscellaneous pile; they should *not* be discarded at this point, but should be retained for later review.

As the process continues in this fashion, new categories will emerge rapidly at first, but the rate of emergence will diminish sharply after some fifty to sixty cards have been processed. At this point certain of the "look/feel-alike" categories will have accumulated a substantial number of cards, say, six to eight, and the analyst may begin to feel pressed to start on the memo-writing task leading to the delineation of category properties and devising of a covering rule [pp. 347–348].

Devising categories involves both convergent and divergent thinking (Guba and Lincoln, 1981). *Convergence* is determining what things fit together—which pieces of data converge on a single category or theme. *Divergence* is the task of fleshing out the categories once they have been developed. In deciding what things fit together, the researcher must also consider the emerging categories. The categories that one constructs should be internally homogeneous; that is, all items in a single category ought to be similar. Categories should also be heterogeneous— "differences among categories ought to be bold and clear" (p. 93).

The number of categories one constructs depends on the data and the focus of the research. In any case, the number should be manageable. In this researcher's experience, the fewer the categories, the greater the level of abstraction. A large number of categories is likely to reflect an analysis based on concrete description. Guba and Lincoln (1981) suggest four guidelines for developing categories that are both comprehensive and illuminating. First, the number of people who mention something or the frequency with which something arises in the data indicates an important dimension. Second, one's audience may determine what is important—that is, some categories will appear to various audiences as more or less credible. Third, some categories will stand out because of their uniqueness and should be retained. And fourth, certain categories may reveal "areas of inquiry not otherwise recognized" or "provide a unique leverage on an otherwise common problem" (p. 95).

There are several guidelines to determine whether a set of categories is complete. First, "there should be a minimum of unassignable data items, as well as relative freedom from ambiguity of classification" (Guba and Lincoln, 1981, p. 96). Moreover, the set of categories should seem plausible given the data from which they emerge, causing independent investigators to agree that the categories make sense in light of the data. This strategy helps to ensure reliability and is discussed further in Chapter Ten.

Once one is satisfied with the set of categories derived from the data, the categories can be fleshed out and made more robust by searching through the data for more and better units of relevant information. Guba and Lincoln (1981, pp. 99-100) list seven guidelines for fleshing out categories:

- Include any information that is germane to the area and not excluded by boundary-setting rules.
- Include any information that relates or bridges several already existing information items.
- Include any information that identifies new elements or brings them to the surface.
- Add any information that reinforces existing information, but reject it if the reinforcement is merely redundant.
- Add new information that tends to explain other information already known.
- Add any information that exemplifies either the nature of the category or important evidence within the category.
- Add any information that tends to refute or challenge already known information.

Much of the work in category construction is a form of content analysis. One is, after all, looking at the *content* of the data in developing categories. Holsti (1969) offers five guidelines by which to judge the efficacy of categories derived from content analysis. The same canons can be applied to categories derived from the inductive comparative strategy used in qualitative data analysis. They are:

1. The categories should reflect the purpose of the research. Sometimes one becomes committed to categories developed early on; care should be taken to ensure that categories are congruent with research goals and questions.
2. The categories should be exhaustive—that is, "all relevant items in the sample of documents under study must be capable of being placed into a category" (p. 99).
3. The categories should be mutually exclusive—no single unit of material should be placed in more than one category.
4. The categories should be independent in that "assignment of any datum into a category [will] not affect the classification of other data" (p. 100).
5. All categories should derive from a single classification principle.

Up to this point the discussion has focused on categories created inductively by the researcher. Although they are not used commonly in qualitative case studies, there are two other strategies for arriving at a set of categories. In the first approach, the data can be organized into a scheme suggested by the participants themselves. "This kind of approach requires an analysis of the verbal categories used by participants and/or staff in a program to break up the complexity of reality into parts. It is a fundamental purpose of language to tell us what is important by giving it a name and therefore separating it from other things with other names" (Patton, 1980, p. 307). Patton gives the example of teachers' classification of dropouts into "chronics" and "borderlines" (p. 308). Bogdan and Biklen (1982, p. 159) found that parents were classified by professional staff as "good parents," "not-so-good parents," or "troublemakers."

In addition to the participants' own categories, classification schemes can be borrowed from sources outside the study at hand. Applying someone else's scheme requires "a compatibility between the research problem posed and the theoretical perspective that informs the strategy" (Goetz and LeCompte, 1984, p. 184). The data base is scanned to determine the fit of a priori categories and then the data are sorted into the borrowed categories. "If the categories sought or discovered in the research site match categories described in the borrowed classification scheme, typologies . . . may be used inductively for both descriptive and generative purposes" (p. 184).

There is some danger in using borrowed classification schemes, however. As Glaser and Strauss (1967) point out: "Merely selecting data for a category that has been established by another theory tends to hinder the generation of new categories, because the major effort is not generation, but data selection. Also, emergent categories usually prove to be the most relevant and the best fitted to the data. . . . Working with borrowed categories is more difficult since they are harder to find, fewer in number, and not as rich; since in the long run they may not be relevant, and are not exactly designed for the purpose, they must be respecified" (p. 37).

Whether the classification scheme originates with the investigator or is borrowed from someone else, the mechanical handling of the data at this stage of the analysis is the same. There are four basic strategies for organizing all the data in preparation for further analysis or for writing the results of the study: index cards, file folders, information retrieval cards, and computer programs.

As described earlier by Guba and Lincoln (1981), units of information can be placed on *index cards*. Each unit of information is coded according to basic identifying factors such as person interviewed, date of observation, and so on. The cards are then sorted into piles by constantly comparing the information on one card with the information on the next. The piles are labeled and the cards within that pile are coded accordingly. Once all the cards have been coded, cards relevant to a certain category can be retrieved by the code on the card.

If *file folders* are used, a photocopy of the entire data base or case record is made. Working page by page, the investigator writes notations in the margins, including tentative categories or themes emerging from the raw data. The photocopied pages are then cut up and coded sections placed into file folders labeled by category or theme. Each unit of data needs to be coded not only by category but by its original page number and possibly by other identifying codes such as respondent's name and so on. If need be, each cut-up piece of information can be located later in the master copy.

There are at least two commercially available *information retrieval card* systems that can be used to sort data (Werner and Schoepfle, 1987). McBee or Indecks cards are large index-type cards with numbered holes around the margins. One first pastes a photocopied unit of data on the card or types the data onto the card. Using the numbered holes, codes are assigned and then the corresponding holes are punched out. Using a large rod somewhat like a knitting needle, one passes it through the hole representing the desired category of all the cards. Lifting and shaking the needle full of cards allows those that have been punched to fall out. One then has all the data pertaining to a specific coded category. Exhibit 5 is an example of an information retrieval card (Indecks) used in a study of displaced workers involved in a retraining program. Note that the unit of

Exhibit 5. Information Retrieval Card.

```
"I was afraid I wouldn't be able to do the
work - you know, keep up with the rest of
the class.  But I've surprised even myself.
Of course it helps having a good teacher
and classmates help.  One stayed late to
help me do  homework and I know she had
little kids to get home to.  If it weren't
for the teacher and other students, I
don't think I could do it."
```

MULTI-PURPOSE DECK   o indecks   ARLINGTON, VERMONT 1969

information on the card has been coded eight different ways: Hole 3 was punched to represent an informant named Sally; hole 7 is for female; hole 18 is for middle age; hole 23 represents experience as an adult learner; hole 25 is coded for feelings of insecurity as a learner; hole 26 is the code for comments about the teacher; hole 34 is for comments about other students; hole 36 is coded for helpful. This technique allows the cards to be left in random order, since all relevant information is coded by using the holes at the edge of the card.

Numerous *computer programs* have been developed to store, sort, and retrieve qualitative data. Some researchers have also devised systems using powerful word processing packages or data base programs. This writer is most familiar with THE ETHNOGRAPH (Seidel and Clark, 1984). Interview transcripts, observation notes, and so on are entered verbatim into the computer. The program then numbers each line of the data base. The researcher uses a hard copy of the numbered data base to analyze the data, making notes in the margins and developing themes or categories. Going from the hard copy back to the computer file, categories and their corresponding line numbers are entered. The researcher can then retrieve and print, by category, any set of data desired. Twelve levels of coding are possible for the same unit of information.

No doubt every researcher devises his or her own scheme for handling qualitative data. The four strategies for sorting data just presented allow for the easy retrieval of data and for cross-analysis of coded categories. Cross-analysis is especially important if one is interested in a level of analysis that goes beyond a categorical or taxonomic integration of the data toward the development of theory.

Developing Theory

Several levels of data analysis are possible in a qualitative case study. At the most basic level, data are organized chronologically or sometimes topically and presented in a narrative that is largely, if not wholly, descriptive. The excerpt presented in Exhibit 4 is from a descriptive case study. Moving from concrete description of observable data to a somewhat more abstract level involves using concepts to describe phenomena. Rather than just describing a classroom interaction, for example, one might cite it as an instance of "learning" or "confrontation" or "peer support" or whatever, depending on the research problem. This is the process of systematically classifying data into some sort of schema consisting of categories, themes, or types. The categories describe the data, but to some extent they also interpret the data. A third level of analysis involves making inferences and developing theory. It is a process, Miles and Huberman (1984, p. 228) write, of moving up "from the empirical trenches to a more conceptual overview of the landscape. We are no longer dealing just with observables but also with unobservables, and are connecting the two with successive layers of inferential glue."

Thinking about one's data—*theorizing*—is a step toward developing a theory that explains some aspect of educational practice and allows one to draw inferences about future activity. Theorizing is defined as "the cognitive process of discovering or manipulating abstract categories and the relationships among those categories" (Goetz and LeCompte, 1984, p. 167). It is fraught with ambiguity. Goetz and LeCompte (p. 198) point out that "going beyond the data into a never-never land of inference" is a difficult task for most qualitative researchers because they are too close to the data, unable to articulate how the study is significant, and unable to shift into a speculative mode of thinking. Theorizing about one's data can also be hindered by thinking that is linear rather than contextual. Patton (1980, p. 325) notes the temptation to "fall back on the linear assumptions of quantitative analysis," which involves specifying "isolated variables that are mechanically linked together out of context." Such noncontextual statements "may be more distorting than illuminating. It is the ongoing challenge, paradox, and dilemma of qualitative analysis that we must be constantly moving back and forth between the phenomenon of the program and our abstractions of that program, between the descriptions of what has occurred and our analysis of those descriptions, between the complexity of reality and our simplifications of those complexities, between the circularities and interdependencies of human activity and our need for linear, ordered statements of cause-effect" (p. 325).

Speculation, however, is the key to developing theory in a qualitative study. Speculation involves "playing with ideas probabilistically. It permits the investigator to go beyond the data and make guesses about what will happen in the future, based on what has been learned in the past about constructs and linkages among them and on comparisons between that knowledge and what presently is known about the same phenomena. These guesses are projections about how confidently the relationships found or explanations developed can be expected to obtain in the future" (Goetz and LeCompte, 1984, p. 173).

The case study investigator who wishes to derive theory from his or her data can turn to Glaser and Strauss (1967) and Strauss (1987) for assistance. They have devised a strategy for developing substantive theory—theory that applies to a specific aspect of educational practice. Since the theory is grounded in the data and emerges from them, the methodology is called *grounded theory.* Much of this chapter's discussion of category construction relates to the development of grounded theory. To begin with, categories are one element of the emerging theory. They should be both *"analytical*—sufficiently generalized to designate characteristics of concrete entities, not the entities themselves," and *"sensitizing*—yield[ing] a 'meaningful' picture, abetted by apt illustrations that enable one to grasp the reference in terms of one's own experience" (Glaser and Strauss, 1967, pp. 38-39). Categories are derived by constantly comparing one incident or unit of information with another, a process described earlier in the chapter.

In addition to categories, a theory consists of two other elements: properties and hypotheses. Properties are also concepts, but ones that describe a category. The category "career malaise," for example, is defined by the properties of "boredom," "inertia," and "trapped" (Merriam, 1980). In a grounded theory study of adult education, the category "domain scope" was defined by the properties of "expansion" and "abridgement" (MacNeil, 1981).

Hypotheses are the suggested links between categories and properties. In a study of a college faculty's participation in in-service workshops, for example, the researcher cited "workshop credibility" as one of several categories explaining faculty participation (Rosenfeldt, 1981). A property that helped to define workshop credibility was called "identification with sponsoring agent." The author hypothesized that "workshop participation will depend on the extent to which faculty members identify with the workshop sponsors. Namely, the greater the identification of the potential participants with the sponsoring agent, the greater the likelihood that professors will participate in a given workshop" (Rosenfeldt, 1981, p. 189). Such hypotheses emerge simultaneously with the collection and analysis of data. The researcher tries to support tentative hypotheses while at the same time remaining open to the emergence of new hypotheses. "Generating hypotheses requires evidence enough only to establish a suggestion—not an excessive piling up of evidence to establish a proof" (Glaser and Strauss, 1967, pp. 39-40).

A variation on Glaser and Strauss's method of developing hypotheses can be found in the strategy called analytic induction (Katz, 1983) or negative-case analysis (Kidder, 1981a). Essentially, the process is one of continual refinement of hypotheses as the researcher finds instances that do not match the original hypothesis. Eventually one evolves a hypothesis that explains all known cases of the phenomenon. The object is to achieve a perfect fit between the hypothesis and the data. Taylor and Bogdan (1984, p. 127) summarize the steps involved:

1. Develop a rough definition of the phenomenon to be explained.
2. Formulate an hypothesis to explain that phenomenon. (This can be based on the data, other research, or the researcher's insight and intuition).
3. Study one case to see the fit between the case and the hypotheses.
4. If the hypothesis does not explain the case, either reformulate the hypothesis or redefine the phenomenon.
5. Actively search for negative cases to disprove the hypothesis.
6. When negative cases are encountered, reformulate the hypothesis or redefine the phenomenon.
7. Proceed until one has adequately tested the hypothesis (established a universal relationship according to some researchers) by examining a broad range of cases.

In a sense this strategy is akin to Glaser and Strauss's (1967, p. 55) recommendation that one should study groups that will maximize and minimize "both the differences and the similarities of data that bear on the categories being studied." Minimizing differences early in the study allows for the establishment of categories and properties. But once the basic framework has emerged, the investigator "should turn to maximizing differences among comparison groups, in accordance with the kind of theory he wishes to develop (substantive or formal) and with the requirements of his emergent theory. . . . Maximizing brings out the widest possible coverage on ranges, continua, degrees, types, uniformities, variations, causes, conditions, consequences, probabilities of relationships, strategies, process, structural mechanisms, and so forth, all necessary for elaboration of the theory" (p. 57).

The development of categories, properties, and tentative hypotheses through the constant comparative method (Glaser and Strauss, 1967) is a process whereby the data gradually evolve into a core of emerging theory. This core is a theoretical framework that guides the further collection of data. Deriving a theory from the data involves both the integration and the refinement of categories, properties, and hypotheses. As the theory solidifies, "major modifications become fewer and fewer as the analyst compares the next incidents of a category to its properties. Later modifications are mainly on the order of clarifying the logic, taking out non-relevant properties, integrating elaborating details of properties into the major outline of interrelated categories" (p. 110). In short, more data can be processed with fewer adjustments because the theory emerges "with a smaller set of higher level concepts" (p. 110). At this point, "with reduction of terminology and consequent generalizing . . . the analyst starts to achieve two major requirements of theory: (1) *parsimony* of variables and formulation, and (2) *scope* in the applicability of the theory to a wide range of situations" (pp. 110–111). Besides parsimony and scope, the emergent theory can be evaluated in terms of its overall explanatory power, by how well the generalizations are supported, by how well integrated the elements are, and by whether there is a logical consistency to every dimension of the theory. Those who build theory in an applied field such as education need also be concerned with how well the theory fits the substantive area to which it will be applied, whether laypersons will be able to understand and use the theory, and whether the person who uses the theory will "have enough control in everyday situations to make its application worthwhile" (p. 245).

While building theory in the manner described by Glaser

and Strauss is largely an inductive process, there are times throughout the investigation when a deductive strategy is used. Tentative categories, properties, and hypotheses continually emerge and must be tested against the data—that is, one asks if there are sufficient data to support a certain category or hypothesis. If so, the element is retained; if not, it is discarded. Thus the researcher is continually shifting back and forth between deductive and inductive modes of thinking. For Glaser and Strauss (1967, p. 28) the difference is one of emphasis: "Verifying as much as possible with as accurate evidence as feasible is requisite while one discovers and generates his theory —but *not* to the point where verification becomes so paramount as to curb generation."

Summary

Analyzing data collected in a case study investigation is tedious and time-consuming work. At best, intensive analysis takes twice the time spent collecting the data. At worst, some researchers find themselves with neither the time nor the energy to tackle the mound of transcripts, field notes, and documents that form the case study data base. Such a situation is especially likely to occur if one has failed to analyze data as they are being collected. Simultaneous analysis and data collection allows the researcher to direct the data collection phase more productively, as well as develop a data base that is both relevant and parsimonious.

Raw data need to be organized in some way. This can be done by arranging transcripts, field notes, and documents chronologically according to when they were collected or according to the logical chronology of the case. All the information related to the planning phase of a project could be arranged first, for example, followed by the implementation phase and so on. Or data could be organized according to persons interviewed, places visited, documents obtained. This body of material forms the case record or case study data base.

Sometimes only a bit more analysis is done in order to determine how best to arrange the material into a narrative account of the findings. The final product then becomes a descriptive case study. A second level of analysis involves developing categories, themes, or other taxonomic classes that interpret the meaning of the data. When categories and their properties are reduced and refined and then linked together by tentative hypotheses, the analysis is moving toward the development of a theory to explain the data's meaning. This third level of analysis transcends the formation of categories, for a theory seeks to explain a large number of phenomena and tell how they are related. A theory grounded in the data also contains elements of control and prediction, both of which can be interpreted in terms of the applied nature of educational research. Educators are knowledgeable, efficient, and even expert in their area. "What a man in the know does not want is to be told what he already knows. What he wants is to be told how to handle what he knows with some increase in control and understanding of his area of action" (Glaser, 1978, p. 13).

CHAPTER 9

Using Special Techniques and Computers to Analyze Qualitative Data

Data analysis is a complex process that involves moving back and forth between concrete bits of data and abstract concepts, between inductive and deductive reasoning, between description and interpretation. Many strategies can be used to make sense of one's data. In the last chapter, we discussed the process of data analysis in terms of what to do while collecting data and how to build categories and theory to interpret the data. This chapter offers further suggestions for deriving meaning from data and deals with how to analyze data in cross-case or cross-site studies. The chapter closes with a brief discussion of the use of computers in qualitative data collection and analysis.

Strategies for Deriving Meaning

Regardless of how well a step-by-step procedure for data analysis is spelled out, there are times when even the most experienced researcher feels deadlocked in the process of analysis. Exactly how a researcher makes sense of data, sees patterns or relationships, or discovers theory cannot be explained as a logical process. There is an element of intuition involved; much depends on the investigator's sensitivity to the data. Intuitive insights do not always come when one wants them to. Breakthroughs in analysis "can come in the morning or at night, suddenly or with slow dawning, while at work or at play (even when asleep); furthermore, they can be derived directly from theory (one's own or someone else's) or occur without theory; and they can strike the observer while he is watching himself react as well as when he is observing others in action. Also, his insights may appear just as fruitfully near the end of a long inquiry as near the outset" (Glaser and Strauss, 1967, p. 251).

The idiosyncratic nature of arriving at insights about one's data precludes presenting a formula for all to follow. What can be offered, however, are some tactics that others have found useful to break through an impasse in the analysis of data. These twelve tactics are drawn from Miles and Huberman's book, *Qualitative Data Analysis* (1984), and are loosely organized from the most concrete technique to conceptual strategies. Some tactics might help in "seeing what's there," some are useful for "seeing things and their relationships more abstractly," and the last two are helpful for assembling "coherent understanding of data" (Miles and Huberman, 1984, p. 215).

Counting. This is an obvious means of finding out "what's there," but it is often ignored by qualitative researchers as being too quantitative. As the authors point out, however, "when we identify a theme or pattern, we are isolating something (a) that happens a number of times and (b) that consistently appears in a specific way" (p. 215). In identifying a property of the phenomenon or making a generalization about a set of data, one decides, "almost unconsciously, which particulars are there *more often*, matter more than others, *go together*, and so on." In indicating that "something is 'important' or 'significant' or 'recurrent,' we have achieved that estimate in part by making counts, comparisons, and weights" (p. 215). There are at least three good reasons for counting something that is found consistently in the data: to get some idea of "the general drift of the data" (p. 215); to test or support or verify an emerging hypothesis; and to protect against investigator bias (pp. 215–216).

Noting Patterns and Themes. Finding patterns in the case study data base is similar to building categories or themes by scanning the data. Explicitly looking for patterns demands a mindset that will allow for unifying constructs to emerge. "The human mind finds patterns so quickly and easily that it needs no how-to advice. Patterns just 'happen,' almost too quickly" (p. 216). The important thing is to notice genuine evidence of the same pattern and remain open to contradictory evidence. Early in Hardin's (1985) analysis of generative midlife men and women, for example, it appeared that each had experienced a pivotal event which caused them to reevaluate their priorities, life-style, and values. This pattern of a pivotal event was confirmed through subsequent data collection and analysis.

Seeing Plausibility. This is essentially an intuitive disposition that allows the researcher to respond to possibilities, hunches, initial impressions, and so on. At first there may be no direct evidence to support a hunch. Miles and Huberman (1984) see plausibility as "a sort of pointer, drawing the analyst's attention to a conclusion that look[s] reasonable and sensible on the face of it" (p. 217). They also note that this can work in reverse —that is, investigators should also attend to the "*lack* of plausibility. When a conclusion someone is advancing 'just *doesn't* make sense,' it's a bit safer to rule it out. But not completely safe. Counterintuitive or puzzling findings can sometimes be extraordinarily stimulating and rich, so they should be allowed their day in the sun too" (p. 218).

Clustering. Clustering is the tactic of grouping together things that appear similar. It can be done on several levels: "at the level of events, of acts, of individual actors, of processes, of settings/locales, of sites as wholes. In all instances we are trying to understand a phenomenon better by *grouping,* then *conceptualizing* objects that have similar patterns or characteristics" (p. 219). At its most basic level, clustering is a sorting process. One asks if two units of information are alike in any way, and thus can be clustered together, or if it makes more sense to separate them. From sorting concrete items into clusters one can move to higher levels of abstraction by analyzing, resorting, and sifting through the clusters themselves. These clusters become the categories and properties of a grounded theory (Glaser and Strauss, 1967).

Making Metaphors. A metaphor is a figure of speech that implies a comparison. A metaphor can convey a lot of information in a few syllables. To say, for instance, that someone is a "team player" implies that the person will cooperate with others and work for the benefit of the group more than for his or her own interests. In education, implied comparisons are commonly drawn from sports ("play the game," "jump through the hoops," "on target," "go to bat," "Monday morning quarterback"), computer technology ("inputs," "outputs"), gardening ("climate setting," "nurture," "grow and develop," "plant the seed"), and business ("bottom line," "consumer," "calculated risk," "product"). Not only can metaphors say a lot without wasting words, but they can add spice to the report when it comes time to write up the final results. A good example of using metaphor to convey research results can be found in *Last Gamble on Education* (Mezirow, Darkenwald, and Knox, 1975) —a large-scale, grounded theory study of urban adult basic education programs. As the title suggests, a gambling metaphor was used to structure the results. Chapters cover "the only game in town," "the players," "the odds," and so on.

In terms of data analysis, thinking metaphorically helps the researcher to rise above the "empirical trenches" (Miles and Huberman, 1984, p. 228) and conceptualize at a higher level. "Metaphors won't let you simply describe or denote a phenomenon, you have to move up a notch, to a slightly more inferential or analytical level. . . . The metaphor is halfway from the empirical facts to the conceptual *significance* of those facts; it gets the analyst, as it were, up and over the particulars en route to the basic social processes that give meaning to those particulars" (p. 221). The trick is to be imaginative.

Splitting Variables. Although analysis is more often thought of as a matter of combining variables, there are times when the data seem to demand that a variable or category be split into two elements. In a study of maladjusted adults, for example, "irresponsible" was a variable that emerged from the interview data to describe their general behavior. Upon further probing, however, it became clear that these adults were irresponsible both socially and physically—that is, they not only failed to handle the responsibilities of adult life but they often reacted to others with physical threats. The variable "irresponsible" thus became split into "socially immature" and "physically irresponsible."

Subsuming Particulars into the General. This tactic is similar to the clustering strategy discussed earlier. It involves asking: "What is this specific thing an instance of? Does it belong to a more general class?" (p. 223). If, for example, an investigator observes a student writing a letter during a lecture, the incident could be subsumed under a general class of behavior labeled "inattention" or "boredom" or "student activity unrelated to lecture" or "coping techniques."

Factoring. Factoring comes from factor analysis, "a statistical technique for representing a large number of measured variables in terms of a smaller number of unobserved, usually hypothetical variables" (Miles and Huberman, 1984, pp. 223–224). Factoring in qualitative analysis is "hypothesizing that some disparate facts or words *do* something in common or *are* something in common. What they do or are is the 'factor.' " A factor is synonymous with a category, theme, or cluster. It is just another way of thinking about how to reduce a large amount of data into meaningful concepts. "The factors have to contribute to our understanding of the case or of its underlying dynamics. Otherwise, they are no more useful than the big, gift-wrapped boxes that unpack into a succession of smaller, but equally empty gift-wrapped boxes, leaving us at the end with a shapeless heap of ribbon and cardboard" (p. 224).

Noting Relations Between Variables. This process involves speculating about how variables or concepts are related to each other. One guesses what sort of relationship exists between two or more conceptual elements in the study. It is essentially the process of developing hypotheses to explain a phenomenon. Miles and Huberman (1984, p. 226) warn that qualitative researchers must be careful not to assume that every relationship between two variables is a causal relationship: "The risk in trying to understand relationships between two variables is jumping too rapidly to the conclusion that A 'causes' B, rather than that A happens to be high and B happens to be high." As when one is developing grounded theory, one needs to seek verification of hypothesized relationships while at the same time remaining open to disconfirming them and evolving new ones.

Finding Intervening Variables. The need to find *intervening* variables arises when two variables that ought to go together do not seem to fit or when two variables go together but it is not clear why or how. "In both of these conditions, looking for *other* variables that may be in the picture is a useful tactic. Perhaps a third variable Q is confusing, depressing, or elevating the relationship between A and B, so that if you 'controlled' for Q, the relationship between A and B would become clearer" (Miles and Huberman, 1984, p. 226). In the study of adult basic education programs mentioned earlier (Mezirow, Darkenwald, and Knox, 1975), it became clear that large programs were more innovative than small ones, but it was not clear *why.* Further analysis pointed to the intervening variable of graduate-trained administrators, which helped explain the relationship.

Building a Logical Chain of Evidence. Building a logical chain of evidence is a strategy for integrating the categories, hypotheses, metaphors, and themes of the analysis into a coherent whole. Miles and Huberman's description of the process recalls the constant comparative method of grounded theory described in the last chapter. According to Miles and Huberman (1984, p. 228), "the field researcher constructs this evidential trail gradually, getting an initial sense of the main factors, plotting the logical relationships tentatively, testing them against the yield from the next wave of data collection, modifying and refining them into a new explanatory map, which then gets tested against new cases and instances."

Making Conceptual/Theoretical Coherence. This tactic, along with the preceding technique, requires a fairly sophisticated level of analysis and interpretation. It is a theory-building activity in which findings are tied together into "overarching, across-more-than-one-study propositions that can account for the 'how' and 'why' of the phenomena under study" (Miles and Huberman, 1984, p. 228). Again, a detailed discussion of theory building can be found in Chapter Eight.

The twelve strategies just presented range from the manipulation of specific bits of information (as by counting) to the formation of integrated theory for understanding the meaning of data. All the tactics are designed to reduce the data gathered in a qualitative case study to a manageable size so that a sense of their meaning can be conveyed to the reader. When these techniques are combined with an intuitive approach to the data, insights and explanations are likely to emerge.

Cross-Case Analysis

The various strategies for deriving meaning from qualitative case study data just described, and the general techniques presented in Chapter Eight, can be used to analyze data from either a single case or multiple cases. As discussed earlier in the book, a "case" is a single bounded system or an instance of a class of phenomena. As Stenhouse (1978) points out, a case is an instance, not a representative, of a class—that is, in the statistical-experimental paradigm one is interested in selecting a sample that is representative of a certain population, whereas a case is selected because it is an example of some phenomenon of interest. In education, the case can be defined in a number of ways—as a person (say, a principal or student), a program (an in-service teacher training program or a reading program), a group of people (teachers, administrators), a movement (back-to-the-basics), an event (graduation), an agency (National Science Foundation), a concept (mainstreaming), or a project (Head Start). One selects a case study approach because of an interest in understanding the phenomenon in a holistic manner. Indeed, there are instances when it is impossible to study a phenomenon in any other way—when, for example, the situation, event, program, or so on is unique or promises to be particularly revelatory.

In a single case study one often samples from subunits within the case in collecting data. As discussed in Chapter Three, the researcher samples subunits, such as people, events, or documents, in a purposeful manner. Cross-case, cross-site, or multisite case studies (terms used interchangeably here) involve collecting and analyzing data from several cases. Instead of studying

one good high school, for example, Lightfoot (1983) studied
six. Her findings are presented first as six individual case studies
(or "portraits" as she calls them); she then offers a cross-case
analysis leading to generalizations about what constitutes a
good high school. Each case in a cross-case analysis is first treated
as a comprehensive case in and of itself. Data are gathered to
learn as much about the contextual variables as possible that
might have a bearing on the case. The data of the single qualitative case are analyzed as described here and in Chapter Eight. If
time, money, and feasibility permit, a researcher might want to
study several cases. In so doing, one increases the potential for
generalizing beyond the particular case. An interpretation based
on evidence from several cases can be more compelling to a
reader than results based on a single instance. "By comparing
sites or cases, one can establish the range of generality of a finding or explanation, and at the same time, pin down the conditions under which that finding will occur" (Miles and Huberman, 1984, p. 151).

A qualitative inductive multicase study seeks to build abstractions across cases. One attempts "to build a general explanation that fits each of the individual cases, even though the
cases will vary in their details" (Yin, 1984, p. 108). The researcher attempts to see "processes and outcomes that occur
across many cases or sites" and to understand "how such processes are bent by specific local contextual variables" (Miles and
Huberman, 1984, p. 151). Glaser and Strauss (1967) point out
that using comparison groups can strengthen a theory. Although
they are speaking of social theory and groups as social units, the
same logic applies in a theory-building cross-case analysis.
Groups, or cases, should be selected for their power both to
maximize and to minimize differences in the phenomenon of
interest. "Comparing as many differences and similarities in
data as possible . . . tends to force the analyst to generate categories, their properties, and their interrelations as he tries to
understand his data" (Glaser and Strauss, 1967, p. 55). George
(1979), in speaking of comparing cases in political science in
order to develop a theory, notes that taking account of unique
aspects of individual cases forces the investigator to develop

more comprehensive theory—"the 'uniqueness' of the explanation is recognized but it is described in more general terms, that is, as a particular value of a general variable that is part of a theoretical framework" (p. 47).

Analyzing data in a qualitative multicase study is identical to analyzing data in a single qualitative case study. The difference is in the *management* of the data; the researcher probably has considerably more raw information and must find ways to handle it without becoming overwhelmed. Cross-case studies are also likely to involve a team of investigators, each studying his or her assigned site. Clearly, then, coordination of both personnel and data is called for. Indeed, ongoing collaboration in data analysis is essential in large-scale studies. Also essential are coordinated systems for recording data. Miles and Huberman (1984) have developed eight methods for analyzing data from several cases or sites. The methods range from simple to complex, from descriptive to explanatory, and all involve devising matrices for displaying data across sites. The problem of assembling data from several cases or sites "coherently in one place . . . is the first deep dive into cross-site analysis. It is also the most important one, since it will collapse the data set into clusters and partitions that will be used for subsequent analyses; this is how the analyst will *see* the data . . . looking at what's there, making sense of it, and trying to sort out the next, most likely, analytic step" (p. 152).

At the most basic level of analysis the authors suggest using an "unordered meta-matrix"—a large chart organized by variables of interest to the researchers that contains bits of narrative such as key phrases, quotes, or other illustrations of the category. From this descriptive display of data from multiple sites or cases, one can advance to higher levels of analysis. That is, the scheme for arranging data can become more and more conceptual—as, for example, arranging data according to a time sequence, according to the degree of the property being discerned, according to what antecedents relate to what outcomes, and so on. At the most abstract level, patterns can be developed to explain the interrelationship of variables. At this level one is engaging in theory building as described in Chapter Eight.

Cross-case analysis, then, differs little from analysis of data in a single qualitative case study. Analysis can be little more than a unified description across cases; it can build categories, themes, or typologies that conceptualize the data from all the cases; or it can lead to building substantive theory offering an integrated framework covering multiple cases.

A variation of cross-case or cross-site studies is the *case survey*. This is a form of secondary analysis in that the case studies surveyed have already been conducted and are available to the researcher. They function as data bases to answer new questions or confirm new interpretations. Stenhouse (1978) has proposed establishing a repository of case records in education so that these data bases can be easily accessed by researchers. In some ways, the Educational Resources Information Center (ERIC) functions as a repository since it contains thousands of documents, reports, and studies in education. It does not separate case studies from other materials, however, so it would take some effort to identify case studies in particular.

The purpose of a case survey is to aggregate "diverse case studies together under a common conceptual framework so that findings will be cumulative . . . to identify what it is we already 'know,' what it is we do not know, and what it is we suspect" (Lucas quoted in Guba and Lincoln, 1981, p. 247). There is a basic strategy for conducting a case survey that differs from data analysis in cross-case studies. First, one has to determine the criteria by which cases are to be selected for analysis. This step requires "a tight definition of the phenomenon under investigation" (Guba and Lincoln, 1981, p. 250). Second, one needs to develop what Yin (1984, p. 117) calls "a closed-ended coding instrument." Coders or reader-analysts apply the instrument to each case, and data are "tallied and analyzed in much the same way as those of a regular survey" (p. 118). Intercoder reliability is assessed, and findings are presented in quantitative form. Although traditional analysis in case surveys and other forms of secondary analysis (see Bowering, 1984) has been quantitative in nature, it is possible to use case study data bases for qualitative analysis. Such an undertaking would be greatly facilitated if there were a case study repository for education from which researchers could obtain the raw information that forms a case record (Stenhouse, 1978).

Computers and Qualitative Data

Cross-site or cross-case analysis involves handling a lot of data from disparate sources, sometimes in conjunction with a team of researchers who may be geographically isolated from one another. The computer has a great capacity for organizing massive amounts of data, as well as facilitating communication among members of a research team—for example, data can be sent directly from an observation site to a central location where other researchers can read the field notes and compare them with their own. Ongoing analysis can be conducted among several researchers almost simultaneously through the use of computers. And by putting data on disks, "we are creating new databases that have the potential to be easily accessible and usable for secondary analysis. This could not only increase the reliability of our studies, but allow a whole new level of secondary analysis. Data from several different field projects could be compared easily" (Conrad and Reinharz, 1984, p. 8).

The use of computers in qualitative data analysis has increased dramatically in recent years (Becker, 1986). Whether the researcher is working collaboratively or individually, the computer has facilitated data management to the point that one has a choice of programs designed for this purpose. This section explains how computers are being used and reviews the advantages and drawbacks of their use in qualitative case analysis.

By far the greatest use of computers is for storing, coding, and retrieving qualitative data for future analysis. Gerson (1984, p. 64) suggests viewing the computer as a very efficient clerk—"one that has a perfect memory, the ability to retrieve any document immediately, and the capacities of an untiring and very fast typist." The ideal computerized clerk accepts instructions from the researcher, performs certain services such as keeping track of where files are located, can be managed by a researcher without much computing knowledge, contains instructions for its use, can provide confidentiality of files, and has a powerful text processing program (Gerson, 1984).

To date, computer analysis of qualitative data is handled in two ways: through word processing or text editing programs or through data base management programs. In the first approach, one can use a word processing package such as WORD-STAR, EASYWRITER, or DISPLAYWRITE or a text editing program such as THE ETHNOGRAPH (Seidel and Clark, 1984) or LISPQUAL (Druss, 1980). The process essentially involves entering verbatim data from interviews, field notes, or documents into a file. Categories describing portions of the data can be identified and entered into the file, as can the investigator's comments, observations, thoughts. Sections of the file can be moved around and organized according to emerging categorical schemes. Text segments with the same identifying codes can be amassed and printed for further analysis. Some programs allow for counting frequencies of a particular word or code and can do quasi-statistical operations. For example, content analysis programs such as the GENERAL INQUIRER (Stone, Dunphy, Smith, and Ogilvie, 1966) or the HARVARD IV PSYCHO-SOCIAL DICTIONARY program can provide ordered frequency lists that might prove helpful in comparative analysis of one's data. Weber (1984) offers a specific example of computer content analysis of the Republican and Democratic 1976 and 1980 party platforms.

But the use of word processing programs or text editing packages is limited to the mechanical operations of handling data. That is, such programs are substitutes for scissors, typewriters, folders, index cards, and so on. They do not analyze or interpret data. The computer can retrieve and display the occurrences of a category, "but it can neither define the category itself nor assess its continuing usefulness. This is a fundamental limitation of the text approach which cannot be overcome. Because data are represented as text, the computer is aware only of their text properties. It is not aware of their properties as objects, categories, concepts, or ideas and it is unable to use those properties to make logical deductions, generalize to other settings, or to perform any of the other tasks which are so important for the interpretation of qualitative data" (Brent, 1984, p. 40).

A second approach to computer analysis of qualitative data is through data base management programs. The essential difference between this approach and word processing is that in this case one creates a system for entering data into a file. The file consists of records containing various *fields*. A data base management program is commonly used for mailing lists, for example. Each address is a record containing fields such as first name, last name, street, city, state, and zip code. Qualitative data could be set up in the same manner. A record with field names appropriate to the context is established and the data entered. Each interview, for example, could be a "record" containing fields related to categories of analysis predetermined by the investigator. A disadvantage of this approach, in contrast to a free-flowing text approach, is that information entered into a data base format must already have been subjected to analysis in order for the fields to be labeled. Furthermore, once the fields have been established and data entered into the record, it is more difficult to conduct continuous data analysis. If one's analysis is far enough along, however, organizing data by record allows for quick and easy retrieval of any part or combination of records that can then be further analyzed. Fellenz and Conti (1987, p. 127) explain how to make use of a word processing program and a data management system *together*. With compatible programs, "the researcher can enter a data set, modify it as needed, rearrange it, print out selected data for further analysis, create new files of the selected data, and incorporate the selected data into the final report."

What Brent (1984) calls *knowledge-based systems* may soon be available to redress some of the limitations of both word processing and data base management approaches. Derived from research on artificial intelligence, knowledge-based systems allow for analogies and inferences to be made about the data. In contrast to traditional programs that "treat the computer as a rather simple-minded clerk who can process a lot of information repetitively to reach a solution, the artificial intelligence approach gives the program a bit more 'common sense,' ... which [allows] it to rule out the obviously wrong solutions and focus on the more promising ones based on useful insights, rules of thumb, or anything else which seems to work" (Brent, 1984, p. 44). Future knowledge-based systems will aid in the analysis and interpretation of data and not simply assist in the mechanical aspects. Brent (1984) lists some of the tasks such programs will be capable of doing:

- Generalization: the ability to determine which properties are shared . . . and so can be represented in the broader concept.
- Empirical analysis of a data base: the ability to scan a data base and "identify interesting relationships, control for possible confounding effects, and draw conclusions from the findings" (p. 48).
- Resolution of conflicting information: the ability to determine which data are incorrect or do not fit the analysis.

Moreover, research in artificial intelligence may make it possible to develop programs that can construct theory, monitor and modify their own operation, act on implicit knowledge, deduce logical implications, utilize analogues, and perform as an expert in certain areas (for example, make a medical diagnosis) (Brent, 1984, pp. 49–50).

Like any other system a researcher might use to organize and manipulate qualitative data, computers have their advantages and disadvantages. Today computers can carry out the tasks of recording, coding, sorting, cross-indexing, and retrieving qualitative data. Those who take the time to learn a word processing/text editing or data management program are rewarded by the speed and flexibility with which data can be organized and retrieved (Gillespie, 1986). The tedium of cutting, pasting, photocopying, and hand sorting is alleviated, thus leaving more time and energy for substantive thinking and analysis. Other advantages to using computers include increased potential for team research and replication. Using a computer forces the researcher to make coding explicit, for example, and can therefore lead to formally comparable results and the accumulation of research findings. There is also, as Weber (1984) notes, "perfect coder reliability in the application of rules for content coding" (p. 128). Conrad and Reinharz (1984) also note the rigor interjected into an analysis based on computer-coded data: "The computer won't miss any piece of coded data and thus makes all examples available to the researcher. This aspect of computer application may enhance the reliability of findings since *all* coded material is presented to the researcher simultaneously for analysis. In addition, it should be possible to easily locate deviant cases, which are often critical in an analysis" (p. 9).

But of course there are limitations in the use of computers with qualitative data. First, there is the cost involved to purchase the equipment or buy computer time from a mainframe. Moreover, it takes time to enter the raw data into a file; unless one has secretarial support for this task, the time might be better spent in analyzing data. In qualitative research, however, it is probably to the investigator's advantage to enter his or her own data so that comments, thoughts, and observations about the data can be inserted as they are being entered.

Another concern in using computers with qualitative data is the effect such technology might have on the process of analysis. Lyman (1984) points out that the writing and reading of field notes is an intimate process that is often self-revelatory. Introducing a computer into the process interjects a different medium and thus a different relationship with one's data. This new relationship is more mechanical and impersonal, perhaps blocking insight that might otherwise emerge. Some of the richness of qualitative data may also be lost if one begins substituting technical language and quantification for description and metaphor. Freidheim (1984, p. 95) also notes the potentially "serious cost of electronic filing" if the file management system determines the choice of topic or type of analysis. There is also the danger of curtailing data analysis if all the information is filed neatly on disks rather than on pieces of paper in front of the investigator. Finally, by having to determine a data filing system early on, category construction and/or theory building may be brought to closure prematurely (Freidheim, 1984).

Summary

The analysis of qualitative data draws as much upon an investigator's creative abilities as upon his or her technical expertise. And, as with any other creative endeavor, the activity can be enhanced by improved technique. This chapter presented Miles and Huberman's (1984) strategies for deriving meaning from data. These tactics, which range from simple counting to more complex theory-building activities, function in several ways: They help the investigator achieve some insights into the data; they help break a deadlock in the process of analysis; and they help reduce the large amount of raw data into manageable proportions.

These techniques, as well as those described in Chapter Eight, can be used in analyzing data across several individual case studies. Cross-case, cross-site, or multi-case analysis proceeds in the same way as in a single case study. The major difference is the amount of data and the number of personnel likely to be involved. The management of both personnel and data needs to be attended to from the outset of the study.

Computers are increasingly being used for the management of qualitative data. There is even a consulting and computer-assisted data processing service, called Quarm, available to qualitative researchers (Tesch, 1986). Most researchers use word processing programs or programs such as LISPQUAL or THE ETHNOGRAPH for qualitative data. Data base management programs and self-designed programs are also in use. Although none of these approaches can perform tasks of analysis and interpretation, artificial intelligence research will surely lead to this capability in the not too distant future. Certainly there are great advantages to using the computer as a data manager or efficient clerk, not the least of which is to facilitate team research and collaboration. Attention still needs to be given to the computer's effect on analysis, though, for we may be in danger of sacrificing the very nature of qualitative analysis in the name of efficiency.

CHAPTER 10

Dealing with Validity, Reliability, and Ethics in Case Study Research

All research is concerned with producing valid and reliable knowledge in an ethical manner. A qualitative case study is no exception. In fact, because of the nature of this type of research, these concerns may loom larger than in experimental designs wherein validity and reliability are accounted for at the start. Furthermore, while there are well-established guidelines for the ethical conduct of research in general, only recently has attention been given to the ethical concerns unique to qualitative research. This chapter explores the issues of validity and reliability and offers practical suggestions for dealing with these issues in a qualitative case study. The chapter concludes by considering the ethical questions likely to arise in qualitative case study research.

Validity and Reliability

In order for a field such as education to learn about itself and conduct its business of teaching children and adults, research studies of all types are regularly undertaken. To have any effect on either the theory or the practice of education, these studies must be believed and trusted; they need to present insights and conclusions that ring true to readers, educators, and other researchers. Research results in education form what Kemmis (1983, p. 106) calls "conceptual stabilities which are platforms for understanding and for action." Kemmis explains how a case study can be both enlightening and activating:

> If case study sometimes provides illumination, it does so because in social life and social science we work pretty much in the dark. . . . Our scientific understandings of social life have all too frequently fragmented it into "manageable" bits which conceal from us the context-embeddedness of social phenomena, their dynamical coherence, their reflexive effects and their true significance which is in action rather than theoretical discourse. Case study, because it is naturalistic, is especially well-placed to make an assault on that fragmentation and its associated obstacles to our understanding. . . . Authentic insights reached through case study have the capacity to work reflexively to change the situation studied. The action-possibilities created by case study are grounded in the situation itself, not imposed from outside it [pp. 108–109].

Cronbach (1975) emphasizes the practical, action-oriented goal for research in a social science such as education versus the amassing of empirical generalizations and laws in the physical sciences. In his view, two types of contribution are possible: One can "assess local events accurately, to improve short-run control," or one can "develop explanatory concepts, concepts that will help people use their heads" (p. 126). Case studies are especially appropriate for meeting both these goals.

The applied nature of educational inquiry thus makes it imperative that researchers and others be able to trust the results of research—to feel confident that the study is valid and reliable. It is hard, however, to assess the validity and reliability of a study without examining its components (Guba and Lincoln, 1981):

It is difficult to talk about the validity or reliability of an experiment as a whole, but one *can* talk about the validity and reliability of the instrumentation, the appropriateness of the data analysis techniques, the degree of relationship between the conclusions drawn and the data upon which they presumably rest, and so on. In just this way one can discuss the processes and procedures that undergird the case study—were the interviews reliably and validly constructed; was the content of the documents properly analyzed; do the conclusions of the case study rest upon data? The case study is, in regard to demonstrating rigor, not a whit different from any other technique [p. 378].

Thus, regardless of the type of research, validity and reliability are concerns that can be approached through careful attention to a study's conceptualization and the way in which the data were collected, analyzed, and interpreted. Different types of research are based on different assumptions about what is being investigated, however, and different designs seek to answer different questions. Thus appropriate standards need to be used for assessing validity and reliability.

Qualitative case study is a particular type of research having its own characteristics and uses as explained earlier in this book. It is a form of what Erickson (1986, p. 119) calls "interpretive" research. Such research is needed in education for several reasons:

1. To make the familiar strange and interesting again—everyday life is so familiar that it may be invisible.
2. To achieve specific understanding through documentation of concrete details of practice.
3. To consider the local meanings that happenings have for the people involved in them—"surface similarities in behavior are sometimes misleading in educational research" (pp. 121-122).
4. To engage in comparative understanding of different social settings—"considering the relations between a setting and

its wider social environments helps to clarify what is happening in the local setting itself" (p. 122).
5.   To engage in comparative understanding beyond the imme-
     diate circumstances of the local setting.

These five reasons for doing interpretive research in education
(rather than searching for general laws or grand theories) reflect
a crucial perspective in assessing the validity and reliability of
qualitative case studies. For if *understanding* is the primary rationale for the investigation, the criteria for trusting the study
are going to be different than if discovery of a law or testing a
hypothesis is the study's objective. What makes experimental
studies scientific or rigorous or trustworthy, for example, "is
the researcher's careful design of contexts of production for
phenomenon (experiments) and the processes of measurement,
hypothesis-testing, inference and interpretation and the like.
What makes the case study work 'scientific' is the observer's
critical presence in the context of occurrence of phenomena,
observation, hypothesis-testing (by confrontation and discon-
firmation), triangulation of participants' perceptions, interpretations and so on" (Kemmis, 1983, p. 103).

Most writers on the topic argue that qualitative research,
because it is based on different assumptions about reality, a different worldview, a different paradigm, should have different
conceptualizations of validity and reliability (Kirk and Miller,
1986). Lincoln and Guba (1985), for example, propose using the
terms *truth value* for internal validity, *transferability* for external
validity, and *consistency* for reliability. In any event, the basic
question remains the same: To what extent can the researcher
trust the findings of a qualitative case study? The following sections address the specific concerns with respect to internal validity, reliability, and external validity and suggest strategies for
dealing with each of these issues in case study research.

Internal Validity

Internal validity deals with the question of how one's
findings match reality. Do the findings capture what is really
there? Are investigators observing or measuring what they think

they are measuring? Ratcliffe (1983) offers an interesting perspective on assessing validity in every kind of research. It should be remembered, he suggests, that (1) "data do not speak for themselves; there is always an interpreter, or a translator" (p. 149); (2) that "one cannot observe or measure a phenomenon/event without changing it, even in physics where reality is no longer considered to be single-faceted; and (3) that numbers, equations, and words "are all abstract, symbolic representations of reality, but not reality itself" (p. 150). Validity, then, must be assessed in terms of interpreting the investigator's experience, rather than in terms of reality itself (which can never be grasped). Furthermore, notions of validity have changed over the years: "In fact, quite different notions of what constitutes validity have enjoyed the status of dominant paradigm at different times, in different historical contexts, and under different prevailing modes of thought and epistemology" (Ratcliffe, 1983, p. 158). Ratcliffe concludes that there is no universal way of guaranteeing validity; there are only "notions of validity" (p. 158). Committing oneself to a particular notion of validity, Ratcliffe (p. 161) warns, can "limit the range of methods that can be applied to pressing problems." As a result, one may be solving the wrong problem (Type 3 error) or solving a problem not worth solving (Type 4 error).

One of the assumptions underlying qualitative research is that reality is holistic, multidimensional, and ever-changing; it is not a single, fixed, objective phenomenon waiting to be discovered, observed, and measured. Assessing the isomorphism between data collected and the "reality" from which they were derived is thus an inappropriate determinant of validity. Then what *is* being observed in qualitative research, and how does one assess the validity of those observations? What is being observed are people's constructions of reality, how they understand the world: "The case study worker constantly attempts to capture and portray the world as it appears to the people in it. In a sense for the case study worker what *seems* true is more important than what *is* true. For the case study worker . . . the internal judgements made by those he studies, or who are close to the situation, are often more significant than the judgements of outsiders" (Walker, 1980, p. 45).

Reality, according to Lincoln and Guba (1985), is "a multiple set of mental constructions . . . made by humans; their constructions are on their minds, and they are, in the main, accessible to the humans who make them" (p. 295). Judging the validity or truth of a study rests upon the investigator's showing "that he or she has *represented those multiple constructions adequately,* that is, that the *reconstructions* (for the findings and interpretations are also constructions, it should never be forgotten) that have been arrived at via the inquiry are *credible to the constructors of the original multiple realities"* (p. 296). The qualitative researcher is interested in perspectives rather than truth per se, and it is the researcher's obligation to present "a more or less honest rendering of how informants actually view themselves and their experiences" (Taylor and Bogdan, 1984, p. 98).

Most agree that when reality is viewed in this manner, internal validity is a definite strength of qualitative research. In this type of research it is important to understand the perspectives of those involved in the phenomenon of interest, to uncover the complexity of human behavior in a contextual framework, and to present a holistic interpretation of what is happening. Goetz and LeCompte (1984, p. 221) discuss four factors that lend support to the claim of high internal validity of ethnographic research:

> First, the ethnographer's common practice of living among participants and collecting data for long periods provides opportunities for continual data analysis and comparison to refine constructs and to ensure the match between scientific categories and participant reality. Second, informant interviews, a major ethnographic data source, necessarily must be phrased close to the empirical categories of participants and are less abstract than many instruments used in other research designs. Third, participant observation—the ethnographer's second key source of data—is conducted in natural settings that reflect the reality of the life experiences of participants more accurately than do more contrived or

laboratory settings. Finally, ethnographic analysis incorporates a process of researcher self-monitoring, termed disciplined subjectivity (Erickson, 1973), that exposes all phases of the research activity to continual questioning and reevaluation.

According to research experience as well as the literature on qualitative research, there are six basic strategies an investigator can use to ensure internal validity:

1. Triangulation—using multiple investigators, multiple sources of data, or multiple methods to confirm the emerging findings. (See Denzin, 1970, for a discussion of triangulation.) This procedure for establishing validity in case studies was cited in an article by Foreman (1948) more than forty years ago. He recommended using independent investigators "to establish validity through pooled judgment" (p. 413) and using outside sources to validate case study materials. In a recent article, Mathison (1988, p. 17) points out that triangulation may produce data that are inconsistent or contradictory. She suggests shifting the notion of triangulation away from "a technological solution for ensuring validity" and instead relying on one's "holistic understanding" of the situation to construct "plausible explanations about the phenomena being studied."

2. Member checks—taking data and interpretations back to the people from whom they were derived and asking them if the results are plausible. Guba and Lincoln (1981) suggest doing this continuously throughout the study. Foreman (1948, p. 414) also recommended this "review by subjects or functionaries" to increase validity.

3. Long-term observation at the research site or repeated observations of the same phenomenon—gathering data over a period of time in order to increase the validity of the findings. (See the discussion of field observations in Chapter Six.)

4. Peer examination—asking colleagues to comment on the findings as they emerge.

5. Participatory modes of research—involving participants in

all phases of research from conceptualizing the study to writing up the findings. (See Merriam and Simpson, 1984, for a discussion of participatory research.)

6. Researcher's biases—clarifying the researcher's assumptions, worldview, and theoretical orientation at the outset of the study.

Reliability

Reliability refers to the extent to which one's findings can be replicated. In other words, if the study is repeated will it yield the same results? Reliability is problematic in the social sciences as a whole simply because human behavior is never static. Even those in the hard sciences are asking similar questions about the constancy of phenomena. Reliability in a research design is based on the assumption that there is a single reality which if studied repeatedly will give the same results. This is a central concept of traditional experimental research, which focuses on discovering causal relationships among variables: "Positivists assume that . . . people's behavior occur[s] as the law-governed result of a concatenation of many antecedent variables. They want to isolate the numerous laws whose operation in conjunction is observable as the flux of behaviors and events. . . . The aim of their research is to establish laws, and to link these laws into a deductively integrated theory" (Halfpenny, 1979, p. 801). Reliability is therefore essential "because of the emphasis on winnowing out causal laws from a maze of uncontrolled variables (society). Without reliability there is no scientific progress toward the accumulation of knowledge about relatively stable causal laws" (Bednarz, 1985, p. 303).

Qualitative research, however, is not seeking to isolate laws of human behavior. Rather, it seeks to describe and explain the world as those in the world interpret it. Since there are many interpretations of what is happening, there is no benchmark by which one can take repeated measures and establish reliability in the traditional sense: "If the researcher's self is the prime instrument of inquiry, and the self-in-the-world is the best source of knowledge about the social world, and social reality is held to be an emergent property of interacting selves, and the meanings people live by are malleable as a basic feature of social life, then concern over reliability—in the postpositivist sense —is fanciful" (Bednarz, 1985, p. 303).

Reliability and validity are inextricably linked in the conduct of research. Guba and Lincoln (1981) make a case for side-stepping reliability in favor of internal validity: "Since it is impossible to have internal validity without reliability, a demonstration of internal validity amounts to a simultaneous demonstration of reliability" (p. 120). Furthermore, findings will be considered more valid by some if repeated observations in the same study or replications of the entire study have produced the same results. This logic relies on repetition for the establishment of truth; but, as everyone knows, measurements, observation, and people can be repeatedly wrong. Scriven (1972) points out that simply because a number of people have experienced the same phenomenon does not make the observations more reliable. All reports of personal experience are not necessarily unreliable any more than all reports of events witnessed by a large number of people are reliable. An audience's account of a magician, for example, is not as reliable as the stagehand who watched the show from behind the curtain.

The notion of reliability with regard to instrumentation can be applied to qualitative case studies in a sense similar to its meaning in traditional research (Lincoln and Guba, 1985). Just as a researcher refines instruments and uses statistical techniques to ensure reliability, so too the human instrument can become more reliable through training and practice. Furthermore, the reliability of documents and personal accounts can be assessed through various techniques of analysis and triangulation.

Because what is being studied in education is assumed to be in flux, multifaceted, and highly contextual, because information gathered is a function of who gives it and how skilled the researcher is at getting it, and because the emergent design of a qualitative case study precludes a priori controls, achieving reliability in the traditional sense is not only fanciful but impossible. Furthermore, for the reasons discussed, replication of a qualitative study will not yield the same results. That fact, however, does not discredit the results of the original study. Several interpretations of the same data can be made, and all stand until directly contradicted by new evidence. In a case study, Walker (1980) points out, "the emphasis is towards '*collecting* definitions of situations' (multiple representations) and the presentation of material in forms where it is open to multiple interpretations. . . . To some extent we are by-passing the usual problems of reliability by passing responsibility for them on to the audience. In other words, the relationship between our representations of events and the events themselves is not critical because no claim is made for our representations as against those made by anyone else" (p. 44).

Since the term *reliability* in the traditional sense seems to be something of a misfit when applied to qualitative research, Lincoln and Guba (1985, p. 288) suggest thinking about the "dependability" or "consistency" of the results obtained from the data. That is, rather than demanding that outsiders get the same results, one wishes outsiders to concur that, given the data collected, the results make sense—they are consistent and dependable. There are several techniques an investigator can use to ensure that his or her results are dependable:

1. The investigator's position: The investigator should explain the assumptions and theory behind the study, his or her position vis-à-vis the group being studied, the basis for selecting informants and a description of them, and the social context from which data were collected (Goetz and LeCompte, 1984, pp. 214–215).
2. Triangulation: Especially in terms of using multiple methods of data collection and analysis, triangulation strengthens reliability as well as internal validity.
3. Audit trail: Just as an auditor authenticates the accounts of a business, independent judges can authenticate the findings of a study by following the trail of the researcher (Guba and Lincoln, 1981). In order for an audit to take place, the investigator must describe in detail how data were collected, how categories were derived, and how decisions were made throughout the inquiry. Essentially researchers should pre-

sent their methods in such detail "that other researchers can use the original report as an operating manual by which to replicate the study" (Goetz and LeCompte, 1984, p. 216).

External Validity

External validity is concerned with the extent to which the findings of one study can be applied to other situations. That is, how generalizable are the results of a research study? Guba and Lincoln (1981, p. 115) point out that even to discuss the issue, the study must be internally valid—for "there is no point in asking whether meaningless information has any general applicability." On the other hand, one can go too far in controlling for factors that might influence outcomes, with the result that findings can be generalized only to other highly controlled, largely artificial situations. For reasons discussed earlier, qualitative case studies usually have high internal validity. The question of generalizability, however, has beset case study investigators for some time. Part of the difficulty lies in thinking of generalizability in the same way as do investigators using experimental or correlational designs. In these situations, ability to generalize to other settings or people is ensured through a priori conditions such as assumptions of equivalency between the sample and population from which it was drawn, control of sample size, random sampling, and so on. Even in these circumstances, generalizations are made within specified levels of confidence.

From this perspective, generalizing from a single case selected in a purposeful rather than random manner makes no sense at all. One selects a case study approach because one wishes to understand the particular in depth, not because one wants to know what is generally true of the many. As Stake (1978, p. 6) observes: "When explanation, propositional knowledge, and law are the aims of an inquiry, the case study will often be at a disadvantage. When the aims are understanding, extension of experience, and increase in conviction in that which is known, the disadvantage disappears."

It has also been argued that applying generalizations to individuals is hardly useful. A study might reveal, for example,

that absenteeism is highly correlated with poor academic performance—that 80 percent of students with failing grades are
found to be absent more than half the time. If student Alice has
been absent more than half the time, does it also mean that she
is failing? There is no way to know without looking at her record. Actually, an individual case study of Alice would allow for
a much better prediction of her academic performance, for then
one would know the particulars important to her situation.

Overall, the issue of generalizability in case study research
centers on whether one *can* generalize from a single case, or
from qualitative inquiry in general, and if so in what way? Those
who view external validity in terms of traditional research design take one of two positions: Either they assume that one cannot generalize from a single case study and thus regard it as a
limitation of the method, or they attempt to strengthen external validity by using standard sampling procedures. Within a single case, for example, one can randomly sample from a subunit
—say, teachers in a school—and then treat the data quantitatively. Another strategy is to use many cases to study the same phenomenon. In multicase or cross-case analysis, the use of sampling, predetermined questions, and specific procedures for
coding and analysis enhances the generalizability of findings in
the traditional sense (Firestone and Herriott, 1984; James, 1981;
Burlingame and Geske, 1979; Yin, 1984).

In situations where multisite studies are impractical or
the phenomenon of interest is unique, the question of external
validity remains: Is generalization from a single case possible?
Only, most writers contend, if "generalization" is reframed to
reflect the assumptions underlying qualitative inquiry. Recon-
ceptualizations of generalizability to be discussed here include
working hypotheses (Cronbach, 1975), concrete universals
(Erickson, 1986), naturalistic generalization (Stake, 1978), and
user or reader generalizability (Wilson, 1979; Walker, 1980).

Cronbach (1975) proposes *working hypotheses* to replace
the notion of generalizations in social science research. He makes
the point that since generalizations decay in time, even in the
hard sciences, they should not be the aim of social science research:

Instead of making generalization the ruling consideration in our research, I suggest that we reverse our priorities. An observer collecting data in one particular situation is in a position to appraise a practice or proposition in that setting, observing effects in context. In trying to describe and account for what happened, he will give attention to whatever variables were controlled, but he will give equally careful attention to uncontrolled conditions, to personal characteristics, and to events that occurred during treatment and measurement. As he goes from situation to situation, his first task is to describe and interpret the effect anew in each locale, perhaps taking into account factors unique to that locale or series of events. . . . Generalization comes late. . . .

When we give proper weight to local conditions, any generalization is a working hypothesis, not a conclusion [Cronbach, 1975, pp. 124–125].

Working hypotheses not only take account of local conditions; they offer the individual educator some guidance in making choices—the results of which can be monitored and evaluated in order to make better future decisions. This practical view of generalization is shared by Patton (1980, p. 283), who argues that qualitative research should "provide perspective rather than truth, empirical assessment of local decision makers' theories of action rather than generation and verification of universal theories, and context-bound information rather than generalizations."

For Erickson (1986), the production of generalizable knowledge is an inappropriate goal for interpretive research. In attending to the particular, concrete universals will be discovered. "The search is not for *abstract universals* arrived at by statistical generalizations from a sample to a population," he writes, "but for *concrete universals* arrived at by studying a specific case in great detail and then comparing it with other cases studied in equally great detail" (p. 130). The general can be found in the particular. Erickson makes this point with regard to teaching:

> When we see a particular instance of a teacher teaching, some aspects of what occurs are absolutely generic, that is, they apply cross-culturally and across human history to all teaching situations. This would be true despite tremendous variation in those situations—teaching that occurs outside school, teaching in other societies, teaching in which the teacher is much younger than the learners, teaching in Urdu, in Finnish, or in a mathematical language, teaching narrowly construed cognitive skills, or broadly construed social attitudes and beliefs. . . .
>
> Each instance of a classroom is seen as its own unique system, which nonetheless displays universal properties of teaching. These properties are manifested in the concrete, however, not in the abstract [p. 130].

Erickson echoes Eisner's (1981) discussion of validity in science and the arts. In Eisner's analysis, the general definitely resides in the particular. And what one learns from a particular situation is indeed transferable to situations subsequently encountered. This is, in fact, how people cope with the world every day.

Drawing on tacit knowledge, intuition, and personal experience is Stake's (1978) notion of *naturalistic generalization*. People look for patterns that explain their own experience as well as events in the world around them. "Full and thorough knowledge of the particular" allows one to see similarities "in new and foreign contexts" (p. 6). This process of naturalistic generalization is arrived at "by recognizing similarities of objects and issues in and out of context and by sensing the natural covariations of happenings" (p. 6). These generalizations develop from experience and, like Cronbach's "working hypotheses," can guide but not predict one's actions.

A fourth way of viewing external validity—one particularly suited to case study research—is to think in terms of the reader or user of the study. *Reader or user generalizability* involves leaving the extent to which a study's findings apply to other situations up to the people in those situations (Wilson, 1979). "It is the reader who has to ask, what is there in this study that I can apply to my own situation, and what clearly does not apply?" (Walker, 1980, p. 34). This is a common practice in law and medicine, where the applicability of one case to another is determined by the practitioner. Wilson (1979, p. 454) proposes "a continuum of usefulness starting within the setting where the information was gathered and stretching to dissimilar settings," because "generalizability is ultimately related to what the reader is trying to learn from the case study." Kennedy (1979, p. 672) contends that the researcher need not be concerned with generalizing—it should be left to those "who wish to apply the findings to their own situations."

To enhance the possibility of a case study's results generalizing in any of these senses (working hypotheses, concrete universals, naturalistic generalization, user generalization), the investigator has to provide a detailed description of the study's context. "The description must specify everything that a reader may need to know in order to understand the findings" (Lincoln and Guba, 1985, p. 125).

In summary, then, depending on one's notion of external validity, the case study researcher can improve the generalizability of his or her findings by:

- Providing a rich, thick description "so that anyone else interested in transferability has a base of information appropriate to the judgment" (Lincoln and Guba, 1985, pp. 124–125)
- Establishing the typicality or modal category of the case—that is, describing how typical the program, event, or individual is compared with others in the same class, so that users can make comparisons with their own situations (Goetz and LeCompte, 1984)
- Conducting a cross-site or cross-case analysis as discussed in Chapter Nine.

Ethics

Concerns about validity and reliability are common to all forms of research, as is the concern that the investigation be conducted in an ethical manner. Early research in both the physical and the social sciences paid little attention to ethical issues inherent in both the production and application of research knowledge. Not until the horror of Nazi concentration camp experiments was revealed, until questions were raised about the uses of nuclear energy, and until physical and psychological abuses of subjects came to light, was the autonomy of researchers called into question. The first set of principles ever established to guide researchers in conducting experiments with human subjects dates to the Nuremberg Code established as a result of the Nuremberg military tribunals of 1945. Since then, many professions have developed codes of ethics pertaining to their field's research activities. Such codes function as guidelines "that alert researchers to the ethical dimensions of their work" (Punch, 1986, p. 37). The ethical code for anthropologists addresses relations with those studied, responsibility to the discipline, to students, to sponsors, and to one's own government and the host government. In psychology and sociology, the codes deal with weighing the costs and benefits of an investigation, with safeguards to protect the rights of participants, and with ethical considerations in presentation of research findings (Diener and Crandall, 1978).

Moreover, the federal government has established regulations to protect human subjects in biomedical, behavioral, and social research. Professional codes and federal regulations deal with issues common to all social science research—the protection of subjects from harm, the right to privacy, the notion of informed consent, and the issue of deception. Federal regulations in particular are somewhat problematic when applied to case study research or other forms of qualitative inquiry because they are based on a model of research in which the definitions of "subject in terms of the relationship between subject and experimenter, of what risk is and when it occurs, and what potential benefits might be, are clear even when not clearly spelled out. The paradigm for such research is medical experimentation. Consequently, it fits smoothly upon some of the more formal and quantitative types of social research, especially psychological experimentation. It fits incongruously, however, upon that variety of research variously known as fieldwork, participant observation or ethnography" (Cassell, 1978, p. 134).

Cassell goes on to consider how the investigator/participant relationship and the risks differ between experimental and ethnographic research designs. In a later work (1982) she proposes a continuum for analyzing risk and benefit in different types of research. At one end is biomedical experimentation, where the investigator has considerable power in various aspects of the study. Other categories, placed in descending order of control, are psychological experimentation, face-to-face surveys, mailed surveys, field or participant observation studies, nonreactive observation, and secondary analysis of data. Obviously, wherever the investigator holds great power and control there is a great danger of abuse and thus a great need for guidelines and regulations. Differences in research design lead to differences in the relative weight of various ethical issues (Cassell, 1982).

In a qualitative case study, ethical dilemmas are likely to emerge at two points: during the collection of data and in the dissemination of findings. Walker (1980, p. 35) lists five specific problems that case study investigators have encountered in conducting research:

- Problems of the researcher becoming involved in the issues, events, or situations under study
- Problems over confidentiality of data
- Problems stemming from competition between different interest groups for access to and control over the data
- Problems concerning publication, such as the need to preserve the anonymity of subjects
- Problems arising from the audience being unable to distinguish between data and the researcher's interpretation

The emergent design of a case study makes it difficult to assess, for example, potential harm to participants. Nor is it always possible to get informed consent ahead of time from participants if one is not certain who will be interviewed or observed. Furthermore, the relationship between investigator and participants changes with growing familiarity and experience with the case.

The standard data collection techniques of interviewing and participant observation present their own ethical dilemmas. Interviewing for a case study—whether it is highly structured with predetermined questions or semistructured and open-ended —carries with it both risks and benefits to the informants. Kelman (1982) describes how the interviewing situation reduces respondents' control over their self-presentation: "The interviewer may not always give them complete information about the study and may ask questions that are indirect or not obviously related to the topic of the interview. . . . Respondents may prefer not to answer certain questions because they are embarrassed about their opinions or their lack of opinions, but they may feel under pressure to respond. Failure to do so would itself be embarrassing because it would both violate the implicit contract they agreed to and reveal something about the areas of sensitivity or ignorance" (p. 80).

In-depth interviewing may have unanticipated long-term effects. What are the residual effects of an interview with a teacher who articulates, for the first time perhaps, anger and frustration with his position? Or the administrator who becomes aware of her own lack of career options through participation in a study of such? Or the adult student who is asked to give reasons for failing to read? On the other hand, an interview may actually improve the condition of respondents when, for example, they are asked to review their successes or are stimulated to act positively in their own behalf.

Observation, a second means of collecting data in a case study, has its own ethical pitfalls depending on the researcher's involvement in the activity. Observation conducted without the awareness of those being observed raises ethical issues of privacy and informed consent. Webb and others (1981), in their book on nonreactive measures, suggest that there is a continuum of ethical issues based on how "public" the observed behavior is.

At one end, and least susceptible to ethical violations, is the public behavior of public figures. At midposition are public situations that "may be regarded as momentarily private" such as lovers in a park (p. 147). At the other end are situations involving " 'spying' on private behavior" where distinct ethical issues can be raised (p. 148).

Participant observation raises questions for both the researcher and those being studied: "Even when participant observers acknowledge their research interest and are accepted on that basis, some reduction in group members' control over their self-presentation may ensue because of the ambiguities inherent in the participant observer role. Group members may come to accept the observers as part of the scenery and act unself-consciously in their presence, revealing information they might prefer to keep private" (Kelman, 1982, p. 86).

The researcher must also be aware of the extent to which his or her presence is changing what is being observed—including the changes taking place within the investigator. Finally, an observer may witness behavior that creates its own ethical dilemmas. What if inappropriate physical contact is witnessed while observing a teacher/pupil interaction? Or documents related to a continuing education program reveal that funds have been misappropriated? Or course-load assignments are based on certain favors being extended? Or a helpless teen is attacked by the group under study? Knowing when to intervene is perhaps the most perplexing ethical dilemma facing case study investigators. "Blanket injunctions such as 'never intervene' offer no practical aid. In the reciprocal relationship that arises between fieldworker and hosts, it seems immoral—and perhaps is—to stand back and let those who have helped you be menaced by danger, exploitation, and death" (Cassell, 1982, p. 156). Taylor and Bogdan (1984, p. 71) conclude that while "the literature on research ethics generally supports a noninterventionist position in fieldwork," failure to act is itself "an ethical and political choice" that researchers must personally come to terms with.

Somewhat less problematic are the documents one might use in a case study. At least public records are open to anyone's scrutiny, and data are often in aggregated (and hence anony-

mous) form. Personal records pose potential problems unless
they are willingly surrendered for research purposes. As for data
collected by other researchers and used in secondary analysis,
the issue here is whether or not the respondent's "tacit consent
to the subsequent analysis can be taken for granted" (Kelman,
1982, p. 81). Kelman believes that it can be taken for granted
and that "serious ethical problems arise only when respondents
agree to provide information for one purpose and the data are
then used for a clearly different purpose" (p. 81).

Analyzing the data one has collected may present other
ethical problems. Since the researcher is the primary instrument
for data collection, data have been filtered through his or her
particular theoretical position and biases. Deciding what is important—what should or should not be attended to when collecting and analyzing data—is almost always up to the investigator. Opportunities thus exist for excluding data contradictory
to one's views. Sometimes these biases are not readily apparent
to the researcher. Nor are there practical guidelines for all the
situations a researcher might face. Diener and Crandall (1978)
offer sound advice to guide one's actions: "There is simply no
ethical alternative to being as nonbiased, accurate, honest as is
humanly possible in all phases of research. In planning, conducting, analyzing, and reporting his work the scientist should strive
for accuracy, and whenever possible, methodological controls
should be built in to help. . . . Biases that cannot be controlled
should be discussed in the written report. Where the data only
partly support the predictions, the report should contain enough
data to let readers draw their own conclusions" (p. 162).

Disseminating findings from a case study can raise further
ethical problems. If the research has been sponsored, the report
is made to the sponsoring agency and the investigator loses control over the data and its subsequent use. Cassell (1978, p. 141)
points out that qualitative research on deviant or disadvantaged
groups "can be used to control those who one studied, or to explain differences between them and the majority," thus providing a rationale for withholding assistance.

The question of anonymity is not particularly problematic in survey or experimental studies where data are in aggre-

gated form. In a case study, however, which by definition is an intensive investigation of a specific phenomenon of interest, it is nearly impossible to protect the identity of either the case or the people involved. Exposure of the case through publication or other means of dissemination poses several risks: the danger of presenting the case in a manner offensive to the participants, "the violation of anonymity, subjecting an individual or group to unwelcome publicity," or "exposing people to legal, institutional, or governmental sanctions because of behavior revealed by the fieldworker" (Cassell, 1978, p. 141). Questions about the researcher's ethical responsibility abound: "Should material be 'cleared' with the group under study, and if so, with which members or factions within the group? How does one weigh the public's 'right to know' against an individual's or group's 'right to privacy' " (Cassell, 1978, p. 141)?

Summary

As in any research, validity, reliability, and ethics are major concerns in a qualitative case study. Every researcher wants to contribute knowledge that is believable and trustworthy. Since a qualitative approach to research is based upon different assumptions and a different worldview than traditional research, most writers argue for employing different criteria in assessing qualitative research.

The question of internal validity—the extent to which one's findings are congruent with reality—is addressed by using triangulation, checking interpretations with individuals interviewed or observed, staying on-site over a period of time, asking peers to comment on emerging findings, involving participants in all phases of the research, and clarifying researcher biases and assumptions. Reliability—the extent to which there is consistency in one's findings—is enhanced by the investigator explaining the assumptions and theory underlying the study, by triangulating data, and by leaving an audit trail, that is, by describing in detail how the study was conducted and how the findings were derived from the data. Finally, the extent to which the findings of a case study can be generalized to other situations—

external validity—continues to be the object of much debate. Working hypotheses, concrete universals, naturalistic generalization, and user or reader generalizability are discussed as alternatives to the statistical notion of external validity, which involves generalizing from a sample to the population from which it was drawn.

Although researchers can turn to guidelines and regulations for help in dealing with some of the ethical concerns likely to emerge in a case study, the burden of producing a study that has been conducted and disseminated in an ethical manner lies with the individual investigator. Even in collaborative research where the "intimacy of a collaborative agreement . . . can foster a comfortable sense of shared, collective responsibility," the individual researcher's accountability is still the "essence of ethical conduct" (Imber and others, 1986, p. 143). No regulation can tell a researcher when questioning of a respondent becomes coercive, when to intervene in abusive or illegal situations, or how to ensure that the study's findings will not be used to the detriment of those involved. The best that an individual researcher can do is to be conscious of the ethical issues that pervade the research process, from conceptualizing the problem to disseminating the findings. Above all, the investigator must examine his or her own philosophical orientation vis-à-vis these issues. Self-knowledge can form the guidelines one needs to carry out an ethical investigation.

CHAPTER 11

Writing the
Case Study Report

For most educators, doing research means designing a study that addresses some problem arising from practice, collecting and analyzing data relevant to the study, and, as a final step, interpreting the results. Often neglected, especially by graduate students who do much of the research in education, is the important step of reporting and disseminating results. The research is of little consequence if no one knows about it. For qualitative research in particular, one of the serious problems is "the point where rich data, careful analysis, and lofty ideas meet the iron discipline of writing" (Woods, 1985, p. 104).

To begin with, emphasis on the investigator as the chief research instrument "tends to make such problems appear more personal than they really are." Second, continuous and simultaneous data collection and analysis "militates against early foreclosure" with regard to findings (Woods, 1985, p. 104). Third, the great amount of qualitative data that must be woven into a coherent narrative makes the task seem especially laborious. Finally, there is no standard format for reporting such data. In a discussion of reporting styles for qualitative research, for example, Lofland (1974, p. 101) writes: "Qualitative field research seems distinct in the degree to which its practitioners lack a public, shared, and codified conception of how what they do is done, and how what they report should be formulated." After reviewing numerous qualitative studies in sociology, Lofland concludes that while all the reports were "alike in their data collection methods and in their employment of qualitative materials," the reports displayed "remarkable diversity" in the style of reporting (p. 109).

This chapter offers suggestions and examples of how to go about presenting the results of a qualitative case study investigation. While such a report can take an oral or pictorial form, the focus of this chapter is on the more common written form of the case study report.

The Writing Process

There is nothing more frustrating than sitting down to a blank piece of paper or blank computer screen and not being able to write. Unfortunately, there is no formula to make this an easy task for everyone. One can take a course in writing, read tips on how to write, talk to those who write a lot—but, like learning to swim, there is no substitute for plunging in and doing it. This is not to say that one should not be prepared and organized for the task. The process of actually writing the case study report can be greatly facilitated by attending to the following tasks prior to writing: assembling the case record, determining the audience, selecting a focus, and outlining the report.

Assembling the Case Record. As discussed in Chapter Eight, data collection and data analysis should be a simultaneous activity in qualitative research. Only by analyzing data as they are being gathered can one organize the data in other than a strictly chronological form. This organization of case study data along the lines of the emerging analysis forms the case record or case study data base. "The case record pulls together and organizes the voluminous case data into a comprehensive, primary resource package. The case record includes all the major information that will be used in doing the case analysis and case study. Information is edited, redundancies are sorted out, parts are fitted together, and the case record is organized for ready access either chronologically and/or topically. The case record must be complete but manageable; it should include all the information needed for subsequent analysis, but it is organized at a level beyond that of the raw case data" (Patton, 1980, p. 303).

A good example of the construction and use of case records prior to writing the case study itself can be found in Rudduck's discussion of her study of teachers as disseminators of action research (1984). Because Rudduck wished to write a case study of the three-year process as a whole rather than a report of each event, she developed case records that became the data base for the case study. She discusses the difference between case study and case record:

> "Case study" is an interpretative presentation and discussion of the case, resting upon evidence gathered during fieldwork. . . . It is a subjective statement which its author is prepared to justify and defend. I was not ready to produce case studies. . . . What I needed was a theoretically parsimonious condensation (Stenhouse, 1978) of the data I collected around each event—a case record (without some condensation, the accumulation of data over time could be overwhelming and physically unmanageable). The case record, then, was a cautiously edited selection of the full data available, the selection depending on the fieldworker's judgement as to what was likely to be of interest and value as evidence [Rudduck, 1984, p. 202].

Before writing the case study, then, one should assemble all the relevant case study data, preferably in case record form— that is, the data must be gone through, culled for extraneous material, and organized in some manner. Most researchers would agree that a well-designed data base is indispensable to the writer.

Determining the Audience. Next the investigator must decide for whom the case report is being written. Schatzman and Strauss (1973, p. 118) call this process *audience conjuring:*

"Since one can hardly write or say anything without there being some real or imagined audience to receive it, any description necessarily will vary according to the audience to which it is directed. Audiences 'tell' what substances to include, what to emphasize, and the level and complexity of abstractions needed to convey essential facts and ideas." Once it is clear who will be reading the case study, the researcher can ask what that audience would want to know about the case. The answer to that question can help structure the content of the report and determine the style of presentation.

The primary audience for a case study report might be the general public, policymakers, the funding source, practitioners, the scientific community at large, or members of the site or project studied. Each audience would have a different interest in the case, requiring a somewhat different approach. Take, for example, a case study of nursing home residents learning to use computers for study and entertainment. The general public via a popular magazine would respond to a human interest report perhaps highlighting one resident's experience. Policymakers, though, are concerned with policy options: "Here the central interest is not in the technical adequacy or intrinsic scientific merit of the study, but in how the study can inform the current decision situation of the policymaker" (Erickson, 1986, p. 153). In the preceding example, policymakers involved in legislation for the aged or nursing home administration might want to know how the program affected the management of staff and residents, whether funding should be channeled into the project, and so on. The funding source for the study—a computer company, for example—would have its own questions, such as how the residents fared with their computers or whether this population represents a market.

Practitioners would be most interested in whether the case sufficiently resembles their own situation to warrant adopting the same practice. "Practitioners may say they want tips," writes Erickson (1986, p. 153), "but experienced practitioners understand that the usefulness and appropriateness of any prescriptions for practice must be judged in relation to the specific circumstances of practice in their own setting. Thus the interest in learning by positive and negative example from a case study presupposes that the case is in some ways comparable to one's own situation." In this example, practitioners in recreation, adult education, and gerontology might be particularly interested in the computer's role in enhancing the residents' ability to learn. Thus the implicit comparison would be between the residents and setting of the study and the residents and setting of the practitioner.

The general scientific community—that is, other researchers interested in the problem of the case study—would need to know the technical aspects of the study, such as how the data were collected and analyzed and what was done to ensure reliability and validity. It is with this information that they would judge the study's value and its contribution to knowledge.

Finally, the study's results might be presented to those who participated. The main concern of participants, Erickson (1986, p. 154) points out, relates to "their personal and institutional reputations." If the findings about residents' use of computers, for example, are to be helpful to the residents and staff, "the reports must be sensitive to the variety of personal and institutional interests that are at stake in the kinds of information that are presented about people's actions and thoughts, and in the ways these thoughts and actions are characterized in the reports" (p. 154).

Determining one's audience should help in defining the relative emphasis of different components of the report. It may be even more helpful to address the report to a particular person in that audience. Spradley (1980, p. 169) quotes advice from an editor regarding a target reader: "Pick out some real person *whom you know*, then set down your materials so this person will understand what you are saying. When you have a 'target reader,' you effect a single level of presentation." Yin (1984, p. 126) suggests not only examining the selected audience closely, but reading other reports "that have successfully communicated with it."

Selecting a Focus. The next step is to select a focus for the case report. The focus depends on the audience for which it is being written, the original purpose of the study, and the level of abstraction obtained during analysis of the data (see Chapter Eight). Bogdan and Biklen (1982) suggest three types of focus: thesis, theme, and topic.

A *thesis* is a proposition put forth to be argued and defended. It often arises out of the discrepancy between what some theory or previous research says should happen in a situation and what actually does happen. Although the literature suggests that matching learning style and teaching style will result in greater knowledge gains, for example, observations of college students might not support such a relationship. Rather, it might be argued that motivation is a more powerful determinant in knowledge gain than matching learning and teaching styles. Because of its argumentative nature, the thesis is a good attention-getting device and particularly suited to popular accounts of research.

Professional audiences and academics are more likely to want a *theme* for a focus. A theme is an overarching concept or theoretical formulation that has emerged from the data analysis. A theme is large enough to hold much of the data collected and analyzed. It is similar to what Lofland (1974, p. 103) calls a frame or "basic structural unit." The frame is general rather than topical in character when it is "brought to a level of abstraction that makes it generally applicable rather than applicable only in a given institutional realm or ideological debate or other localized concern" (p. 103). The theme that runs through Kline's case study of a back-to-industry program, and which served to structure the report, is that *both* industry and faculty accrued benefits from participating in the program (Kline, 1981).

The third type of focus discussed by Bogdan and Biklen (1982) is the *topic.* This focus is descriptive rather than conceptual and tends to deal with a specific aspect of the study. "What is a good teacher?" is an example. A topical focus is likely to have the most appeal to practitioners.

Bogdan and Biklen (1982) point out that in reality the three types of focus—thesis, theme, and topic—are often blended in the same research report. The important thing is that *some* focus be chosen for the study. As Spradley (1980, p. 169) says:

"In order to communicate with your audience you need to have something to say. . . . A thesis is the central message, the point you want to make." Thus the focus depends on the audience one is addressing and the message the researcher wants to convey.

Outlining the Report. Assembling the case record, determining the audience, and selecting the focus of the report leads easily to the next step: outlining the report. An easy way to outline is to write down all the topics that might be covered in the report. Next arrange the topics in some sort of order that will be understood by the intended audience. All case study reports need an introduction defining the problem that was studied, describing the case, and, depending on the audience, giving information about the methodology. The main body of the report contains the findings in the form of topics that have been listed and organized in some way. A conclusion summarizes the study and its findings and perhaps offers some commentary on the findings. Patton's outline for a qualitative evaluation study is equally applicable to a case study report. Major components of the outline suggested by Patton (1980, pp. 340–342) are:

1. Purpose of the evaluation—describing the context of the study and its particular focus
2. Methodology—discussing the appropriateness of the methods selected and explaining how design and sampling decisions were made
3. Presentation of the data—describing the program and analysis of data presented as patterns, themes, and categories and interpreting the findings
4. Validation and verification of the findings—discussing the credibility of the findings and explaining what was done to ensure reliability and validity
5. Conclusions and recommendations

Beginning to Write. From the outline, one can begin to write the first draft of the report. By breaking the task into manageable units vis-à-vis the outline, one is not so likely to be overwhelmed. As stated earlier, there is no substitute for actually *writing*—all the preparation in the world does not save one from having to put words on paper or characters on a screen. The act of writing itself causes something to happen: "It seems, in fact, that one does not truly begin to think until one concretely attempts to render thought and analysis into successive sentences" (Lofland, 1971, p. 127). It is the combination of thinking while writing that leads to seeing new ideas or revising the outline when certain sections do not make sense. "One is never truly inside a topic—or on top of it—until he faces the hard task of explaining it to someone else. It is in the process of externalizing (writing) one's outline descriptions, analyses, or arguments that they first become visible to oneself as 'things' 'out there' that are available for scrutiny. When they become available as external objects—as text—one can literally see the weaknesses—points overlooked, possibilities unattended, assertions unsupported or unillustrated" (Lofland, 1971, p. 127).

All writers occasionally experience writer's block. Lofland (1971, p. 127) suggests that it is probably more accurately a "thinking block." And while organization and outlines are important and helpful, "one can also become a prisoner of his organization" (p. 128). If writer's block occurs, one can try several tactics. First, writing *anything* is better than not writing. The material may or may not be used later, but forcing oneself to write something may trigger more thinking and writing. A second suggestion is to set deadlines for completing a certain number of pages and meet these deadlines no matter what is written. Werner and Schoepfle (1987, p. 297) suggest shifting to a different medium of communication—writing a letter about the research to a friend, for example, or giving a talk, formal or informal, on the topic. A tape recording of the lecture or conversation can later be used as a stimulus for writing.

The first draft of the case report is just that: a first draft. No matter how rough or disjointed some sections may be, it is infinitely easier to work from something than to be thinking only about what *might* be written. The first draft can be given to colleagues, friends, or participants for comments. Incorporating their suggestions with one's own editing will result in a more refined draft that may be close to the final version. In any case, writing the initial draft is the most laborious and time-consuming phase. Successive revisions are much less tedious; gradually the report takes shape and one can feel a sense of accomplishment as the research process comes to a close.

In summary, then, the actual writing of a case study can be made easier by breaking the task into smaller steps. According to Werner and Schoepfle (1987, p. 302), "planning is the most important part of writing." With a well-thought-out strategy for tackling the case study report, it becomes a manageable undertaking. One such strategy has been suggested here. First, assemble all the materials related to the case in an organized fashion. Second, determine the intended audience, since different audiences will be interested in different questions and components of the study. Third, select a focus that meets the interest of the intended audience and addresses the original purpose of the study. Fourth, outline the report once the central message has been determined. Finally, begin writing. The outline may be refined, adjusted, or revised entirely to coincide with the thoughts and ideas one has while writing. It is wise to have others read the first draft before undertaking revisions that lead to the final form of the report.

Content of the Case Study Report

The first part of this chapter has dealt with the writing process itself and how one can organize the undertaking to produce a case study report for dissemination. This section addresses some of the questions case study investigators face regarding the actual *content* of the case study. What are the components of a case study report? Where should the methodology, references to other research, data displays, and such be placed in the report? How does one integrate description with analysis, and how can some balance be maintained between the two? Also discussed are other formats for reporting and disseminating a case study report.

Components of a Case Study Report. There is no standard format for reporting case study research. Diversity in style of reporting qualitative research is "rampant" according to Lofland (1974, p. 110). The contents of a case study report depend on the audience's interest as well as the investigator's purpose in doing the research in the first place. Practitioners or the general public, for example, will not be much interested in methodological information, whereas colleagues and other researchers will find such information crucial for assessing the study's contribution to the field. In this discussion, we assume that the case study is to be written for graduate students, colleagues, researchers, and/or scholarly practitioners in education. Variations on the basic structure can be made for other audiences.

All case reports discuss the nature of the problem investigated, the way the investigation was conducted, and the findings that resulted. Lincoln and Guba (1985, pp. 362–363) list five basic elements of the substantive part of a case study and three elements related to the methodology. Substantively, a case study report should contain:

- A discussion of the problem which gave rise to the study.
- "A thorough description of the context of setting within which the inquiry took place and with which the inquiry was concerned. This is one of the two items that make up the bulk of the 'thick description.' "
- "A thorough description of the transactions or processes observed in that context. . . . This is the other item involved most closely in thick description."
- A discussion of the key elements that are studied in depth.
- "A discussion of outcomes of the inquiry which may most usefully be thought of as the 'lessons to be learned' from the study. The reader should carefully note that these lessons are *not* generalizations but 'working hypotheses' that relate to an understanding of the site" (p. 362).

The methodology sections should contain, first, information about the investigator including training, experience, philosophical orientation, and "biases toward the problem or setting" (p. 363); second, a description of the methods used to collect and analyze data; and third, "a thorough description of the

measures that were taken to increase the probability of a trustworthy study" (p. 363).

Placement of Component Parts. Where should one place
the methodology section, the references to previous research
and literature, and the visual displays? Again the answer depends on the sophistication and interest of the target audience.
For most audiences, the three-part methodology section listed
above would be placed in an appendix to the case study report.
Referring to an ethnographic study, Werner and Schoepfle
(1987, p. 282) write: "The average reader is not interested in
how the ethnography was obtained as long as he or she retains
a feeling for the quality, validity, and reliability of the monograph. On the other hand, for fellow ethnographers a methodological section may be of great importance. Under no circumstances should it be left out, but its placement should be
dictated by the anticipated readership."

Case studies in professional journals present a discussion
of methodology early in the article—often as part of the introduction of the problem or immediately following it. Boggs's
(1986) article reporting the results of a case study of the educational activities of a local citizens group called HART (Huron
Agricultural Resources Tomorrow) summarizes the problem as
follows: "The HART case study provides an opportunity for exploring (a) criteria to guide adult educators in determining
whether to assist citizen groups who combine education with
social action and (b) the forms of assistance a citizen group
might welcome most from an adult education agency" (p. 2).
The problem is then followed by a two-page review of relevant
literature. The methodology section consists of a one-page explanation of how the case study was chosen and how data were
gathered. Here is an excerpt from the methodology:

> A case study . . . is a detailed examination of one
> setting, one single subject, one single depository of
> documents, or some particular event. Several the-
> oretical perspectives and several disciplines can pro-
> vide the basis for such a detailed examination. . . .
> The focus of this examination . . . was on the self

and community education efforts undertaken by HART to achieve its objectives.

Four sources of data were relevant in this case study. First, HART leaders and members were interviewed over a period of eight months. These persons were asked to describe the HART experience—its origins, purposes, activities, successes, and failures. They were asked to elaborate on the measures taken to educate themselves and the Harbor Beach community on the power plant initiative. The chairperson of the education committee was interviewed twice. Second, a scrapbook of newspaper clippings chronicled the public story. The scrapbook presented the perspectives of HART, Detroit Edison, elected officials, government agency personnel, the newspaper editor, and the general public in letters-to-the-editor. . . . A third data source was the newsletter published every two months for distribution to the HART membership. . . . A fourth source of data was the educational materials prepared by HART. . . . The period of time in which data were collected and analyzed was roughly Autumn 1979 to Spring 1982 [Boggs, 1986, p. 5].

Where should one refer to literature relevant to the problem being studied? This question too may be of concern. In experimental or survey research, a review of previous research and writing is part of the introduction and development of the problem. Glaser (1978) argues for a much later handling of relevant literature in grounded theory studies so the researcher will not be unduly influenced by others' ideas regarding the problem under study. In this way one can remain open to discovering new insights. Lincoln and Guba (1985, p. 369) raise an interesting question: "If the literature is to be critiqued via the case, should not the case writer know in what sense, so as to be sure to include materials that would make such a critique possible?" Thus if the case study is being undertaken as a critique of some theory, principle, or accepted piece of folk wisdom, the investigator should establish that fact with appropriate reference to the literature early in the case study report. On the other hand, if someone else's categorical scheme is being used to interpret the data collected (rather than evolving one from the data), such references should be made just prior to use of the material. Finally, discussion of the study's findings might very well incorporate references to other reports in pointing out where the study's findings deviate from previous work or support it.

Thus references to relevant literature can be placed early in the report when describing the problem, in a section reviewing previous work, or in the section devoted to presentation and interpretation of the study's results. Keep in mind the intended audience and the desired length of the report when making this decision.

What about charts, tables, and figures? Their placement must also be considered in writing the final report. Miles and Huberman (1984, p. 21) make a strong case for creating data displays to help analyze one's data and communicate findings. "Better displays," they write, "are a major avenue to valid qualitative analysis." Displays "are designed to assemble organized information in an immediately accessible, compact form, so that the analyst can see what is happening and either draw justified conclusions or move on to the next-step analysis the display suggests may be useful" (pp. 21–22). They note that the typical mode of displaying qualitative research has been through words in a narrative text. Used by itself, narrative text is an "extremely weak and cumbersome form of display" that is hard on both analysts and readers. For policymakers in particular, "narrative text case studies are almost useless" due to lack of the "time and energy required to comprehend a long account and draw conclusions for their work" (p. 79).

Displaying qualitative case study in the form of a chart, matrix, table, or figure has several advantages: "The analyst can *eyeball* the table to see where the common threads and contrasts are. The table also allows for a more *refined analysis* and can lead to *new displays and analyses*. The table can be *compared with other, similarly formatted tables*—those for the same site, but during other time periods, and those from other sites. Finally, the table can figure in a case *report*, with a short interpretive analysis and commentary attached" (Miles and Huberman, 1984, p. 80).

In deciding to use tables and figures, keep in mind Van Dalen's (1966, p. 431) observation that their use is recommended "only if it snaps important ideas or significant relationships into sharp focus for the reader more quickly than other means of presentation." In using visual displays in a case study report, one should:

- Keep the display simple, including only the information that is necessary to understanding the presentation.
- Keep the number of displays to a minimum. Using just a few figures to represent important ideas will draw attention to those ideas.
- Mention the display in the text, keeping the display as close to its discussion as possible.

Displays should be an *integrated* part of the case study narrative. That is, displays introduced in a sentence or two leave too much interpretation up to the reader. The researcher must at least explain how the data displayed in the table or figure or chart illustrate some aspect of the case, whether it is descriptive or interpretive information.

Description and Analysis. One of the most difficult dilemmas to resolve in writing a case report is deciding how much concrete description to include versus analysis and interpretation. A corollary problem is how to integrate one with the other so that the narrative remains interesting and informative. Lofland's (1974) review of styles of reporting qualitative field research found that some writers' presentations of supporting data amounted to overkill: "Inflicted unedited upon readers, four or five page extracts are used to illustrate single points" (p. 104). At the other extreme were writers so enamoured with the conceptual frame of their study that "the actual report emerge[s] more or less divorced from the adequate empirical materials—direct quotes and direct descriptions—remaining in the field worker's files" (p. 108). Reviewers of qualitative sociology reports, Lofland writes, have a rule of thumb that "sixty to seventy percent of the report is events, anecdotes, episodes, and the like, and some thirty to forty percent is conceptual framework" (p. 107). Strauss (1987) makes the point that a case study that builds theory will understandably rely more heavily on analytic commentary than on raw data.

Whether this 60/40 or 70/30 split is a good guideline for writing qualitative case studies in education remains to be tested by checking what in fact gets accepted for publication in the field. The discussion does, however, point to a real problem in writing the results of a case study. A case report, it might be recalled, is an interpretive presentation of data collected on some phenomenon of interest. "The case study," Patton (1980, p. 304) writes, "should take the reader into the case situation, a person's life, a group's life, or a program's life." Detailed description of particulars is needed so that the reader can vicariously experience the setting of the study; detailed description is also necessary for the reader to assess the evidence upon which the researcher's analysis is based.

At the same time, order needs to be imposed on the details so that readers come to understand what the researcher has learned. "Descriptive excess is the practice of becoming so engrossed in the rendering of concrete details of a setting that one loses connection with any analytic categories and concepts that help to order, explain, or summarize the concrete details" (Lofland, 1971, p. 129). Lofland discusses the "agony"of omitting material to avoid descriptive excess: "Unless one decides to write a relatively disconnected report, he must face the hard truth that no overall analytic structure is likely to encompass every small piece of analysis and all the empirical material that one has on hand. Decisions to drop some things must be made. This, however, does not mean that such topics are lost forever. They can be dealt with in separate papers or even separate books. One decides that for the purposes of *this* report, inclusion within the context of a given overall structure is not coherently feasible" (1971, p. 123).

Chapter Eight of this book discusses the process of analyzing data beginning with the data collected from interviews, observations, and documents. One can present a basically descriptive narrative account of the data organized in a logical fashion; one can build conceptual categories or explanatory concepts that encompass much of the raw data; or one can develop an integrated framework or theory about the phenomenon under study. In a somewhat similar fashion, Erickson (1986) discusses the process of data analysis but points out that the units in the process "are also the basic elements of the written report of the study" (p. 149). That is, the raw data are reported as particular description, patterns discovered in the data are reported as general description, and ever higher levels of abstraction become interpretive commentary: "Such commentary is interpolated between particular and general description to help the reader make connections between the details that are being reported and the more abstract argument being . . . reported" (p. 149).

Particular description consists of quotes from people interviewed, quotes from field notes, and narrative vignettes of everyday life "in which the sights and sounds of what was being said and done are described in the natural sequence of their occurrence in real time" (Erickson, 1986, pp. 150–151). *General description* is needed to tell the reader whether the vignettes and quotes are typical of the data as a whole. "Failing to demonstrate these patterns of distribution—to show generalization *within the corpus*—is perhaps the most serious flaw in much reporting of fieldwork research" (Erickson, 1986, p. 151). *Interpretive commentary*, the third element in a case study report, provides a framework for understanding the particular and general descriptions just discussed: "The interpretive commentary that precedes and follows an instance of particular description is necessary to guide the reader to see the analytic type of which the instance is a concrete token. . . . Interpretive commentary thus points the reader to those details that are salient for the author, and to the meaning-interpretations of the author. Commentary that follows the particular vignette or quote stimulates the retrospective interpretation of the reader. Both the anticipatory and the subsequent commentary are necessary if the reader is not to be lost in a thicket of uninterpretable detail" (Erickson, 1986, p. 152).

Erickson recognizes the difficulty of alternating between "the extreme particularity of detail found in the vignette (or in an exact citation from fieldnotes or in a direct quote from an interview) and the more general voice of the accompanying interpretive commentary" (p. 152). Report writers tend to err in presenting too much description or "adopting a voice of medium general description—neither concrete enough nor abstract enough" (p. 152). Since there are no set guidelines on how to achieve the right balance between the particular and the general, between description and analysis, the case study investigator usually learns how to balance the two through trial and error. One might also read exemplary case reports (see Strauss [1987], pp. 224–240) and consult experienced colleagues to learn how to balance description versus analysis.

A common format for integrating concrete description and interpretive commentary is to follow the introduction of the problem and description of the case with an overview of the structure into which the data have been organized. Parts of the structure, typology, or theory are then presented in a detailed discussion and supported by vignettes and quotes. In a study of good high schools, Lightfoot (1983, p. 96) illustrates, with a vignette, how one attendance officer "rearranges the traditional patterns of power and exchange" between the school and poor minority parents. The vignette also illustrates "his honor of parents, his integration of empathy and toughness, his belief in the capacities of each individual student" (p. 96):

> At Epstein's desk a quiet, shy Black boy is trying to get permission to reenter school after several weeks of absence. His mother has been in a serious car accident and since her hospitalization, he has not come to school. The boy, who is frail and awkward, looks strikingly vulnerable and Epstein's tone seems to noticeably soften. A call is made to the boy's aunt who is at work. "I'm going to dial the number," says Epstein, "but you say hello to your aunt, so she won't get scared. Tell her it's Mr. Epstein from the attendance office. Then I'll talk to her." The boy repeats Epstein's words ver-

batim and hands the phone across the desk to him.
Epstein is gentle and respectful. "Hello, how are
you? We wanted to call to confirm Robert's absences. He has been absent a lot and we've received
no notes from home. . . . He'll fail his subjects unless we hear from you confirming his absences."
There is a long pause in which the aunt must be
offering an explanation. Epstein follows with a
few questions and then closes by saying, "Okay,
we'll try to help him. He seems like a nice boy.
Take care now and thanks for your time." Robert
has been on the edge of his chair, his body erect
and tense, during the telephone conversation. His
eyes search Epstein's face. Epstein returns his full
gaze and says with a stronger voice, "Let me tell
you something important. What happened to your
mom is very serious. No doubt about it. It was very
scary, extremely frightening . . . but rather than be
absent through all of the hard times, you must
come to school. Come here and we'll talk about it.
. . . Just think, if Mom comes out of the hospital
and you've failed your subjects, she's going to be
very sad and disappointed. . . . There are lots of
people around here who you can get to know, who
could care about you. But you have to be in
school." . . . Robert seems to hang on each word
and looks comforted, not chastised [Lightfoot,
1983, p. 99].

For an example of how one follows an observation or interpretive summary statement with direct quotes, consider the
following excerpt from a case study of how setting (in this case,
the home) affects the teaching/learning transaction:

Several teachers told us how they were keenly aware
of changes in their manner of teaching stemming
essentially from the setting. For instance one said:
"In the homes I find that time must be allowed for

chitchat with students, while in the classroom I
don't find this happening. You see the way we
usually lecture in the classroom just isn't suitable
in a home. I find it more natural and effective to
be just very informal." Another teacher said: "I
find that in their homes my students don't get as
uptight as they do in the school. The formal classroom, your tests, the rows of desks, and the like, I
think make adult students very self-conscious"
[Driessen and Pyfer, 1975, p. 115].

One might also weave together a direct quote or description with an assertion or interpretive statement, as in the following example from a case study evaluation of a federally supported project at a private junior college:

Two further points should be made about the students' stated levels of satisfaction. The first is that,
as a group, they are not very vocal, and the second
is that they are busy. As one nineteen-year-old
Physical Therapy student said when I asked about
extracurricular activities and student involvement
in government, "We're too busy. Anyway, in your
first year you're new and in your second year
you're gearing up to start work." Sandra Bailey, a
counselor, suggested that students were not too in-
clined to analyze their situations, implying that it
was partly their personal style. She added that student workloads were well-matched to the time
available and that students found the work demanding [Malcolm and Welch, 1981, p. 28].

How one integrates data to support the analysis and interpretation is not as important as achieving some balance between
the two. No case study report should be all empirical data or all
theoretical analysis. It is the *mixture* that conveys to the reader
the researcher's interpretation of the case and the basis for that
interpretation. "The job involves deciding which evidence to use

to illustrate your points; it is a balancing act between the particular and the general. Your writing should clearly illustrate that
your abstract ideas (actually summaries of what you saw) are
grounded in what you saw (the details that, taken together, add
up to the generalization). . . . Your task is to convince the reader of the plausibility of your presentation" (Bogdan and Biklen,
1982, pp. 176–177).

   Disseminating the Case Study Report. Depending on the
study's sponsor, its purpose, and the intended audience, the format used in reporting the results can vary. For certain groups
one might consider writing executive summaries or specialized
condensations. Another suggestion is to replace the narrative
with a set of open-ended questions and answers drawn from the
data (Yin, 1984). This format is particularly useful for reporting multiple-case studies: "A reader need only examine the answers to the same question or questions within each case study
to begin making cross-case comparisons. Because each reader
may be interested in different questions, the entire format facil-
itates the development of a cross-case analysis tailored to the
specific interests of its readers (Yin, 1984, p. 129). Still another
possibility is to prepare analytic summaries with supporting
data in appendixes (Rist, 1982).

   Patton (1980) even questions the need for a final report
in case studies, especially those with a focus on evaluation. He
has found that final reports "have less impact than the direct,
face-to-face interactions" with those interested in using the results of the evaluation. In his opinion, "the burden of proof lies
with the decision makers and information users to justify production of a full report" (p. 340). Certainly oral delivery in the
form of conference presentations, debriefings, press conferences, and the like serves the purpose of communicating and
disseminating the results of case study research. In fact, a case
study could be presented in the form of film, videodisk, or pictorial display.

   Most researchers are interested in disseminating the results of their case studies beyond a sponsor and participants.
Such dissemination is done primarily through conferences or
journals in the field. Conferences are organized by professional

associations, institutions, and agencies and are usually open to anyone interested in the topic. Any conference is an avenue for disseminating the results of one's research—depending on the conference's goals and whether or not one can frame the report in terms of those goals. A case study on teachers' influence on social studies curriculum, for example, could be presented at a conference on research, curriculum issues, teaching, or social studies.

Publishing the case study report in a professional journal means familiarizing oneself with the journal's format, style, procedures for submission, and focus. There is no point in sending a case study to a journal that publishes only experimental research, even if the topic matches the journal's content. Since there is wide diversity in case study reporting, it is a good idea to find a case study or two in the journal to serve as prototypes. Most fields of education—curriculum and supervision, science education, adult education, and so on—have at least one journal that will consider qualitative research for publication. Journals in related fields such as anthropology, sociology, and psychology might also publish case studies dealing with educational issues.

Other modes of dissemination might be through the in-house publications of professional associations, foundations, social service agencies, and community organizations. And, of course, case studies sometimes get published in book form. Often such books are produced by presses associated with the university or organization where the study was done. Occasionally, a commercial press will publish research results that have wide appeal (Neustadt and Fineberg's 1983 case study of the Swine Flu epidemic, for example).

Summary

This chapter has focused on the writing of a case study report. Without the important step of reporting and disseminating results, the research process would not be complete. Research in education is important for extending the knowledge base of the field as well as for understanding and improving practice.

Case study research can contribute to both theory and practice, but only if it is communicated beyond the research situation. Several suggestions were made with regard to actually writing the case report. First the writer should compile all the data relevant to the case and then determine the intended audience. The next step is to settle on the main message one wishes to communicate—that is, the focus or theme of the study. An outline reflecting the study's focus is essential for dealing with a large amount of material. One is then ready to write the first draft. Peers, participants, and colleagues should all be asked to review the draft before the writer attempts a revision.

What makes an exemplary case study? Yin's answer provides five important criteria, most of which have been dealt with explicitly or implicitly in this chapter:

- The case study must be significant.
- The case study must be complete.
- The case study must consider alternative perspectives.
- The case study must display sufficient evidence.
- The case study must be composed in an engaging manner (Yin, 1984, pp. 140–145).

By paying attention to these criteria in composing the case study report, the researcher will be making a contribution not only in terms of the study's content but in terms of case study as a research genre having its own form of reporting.

REFERENCES

Adelman, C., Jenkins, D., and Kemmis, S. "Rethinking Case Study: Notes from the Second Cambridge Conference." In *Case Study: An Overview.* Case Study Methods 1 (Series). Victoria, Australia: Deakin University Press, 1983.

Altheide, D. L. "Ethnographic Content Analysis." *Qualitative Sociology,* 1987, *10* (1), 65–77.

Becker, H. S. "Social Observation and Social Case Studies." In *International Encyclopedia of the Social Sciences.* Vol. 11. New York: Crowell, 1968.

Becker, H. S. "Teaching Fieldwork with Computers." *Qualitative Sociology,* 1986, *9* (1), 100–103.

Bednarz, D. "Quantity and Quality in Evaluation Research: A Divergent View." *Evaluation and Program Planning,* 1985, *8,* 289–306.

Bogdan, R. C. *Participant Observation in Organizational Settings.* Syracuse: Syracuse University Press, 1972.

Bogdan, R. C., and Biklen, S. K. *Qualitative Research for Education: An Introduction to Theory and Methods.* Newton, Mass.: Allyn & Bacon, 1982.

Boggs, D. L. "A Case Study of Citizen Education and Action." *Adult Education Quarterly,* 1986, *37* (1), 1–13.

Bowering, D. J. (ed.). *Secondary Analysis of Available Data Bases.* New Directions for Program Evaluation, no. 22. San Francisco: Jossey-Bass, 1984.

Brandt, R. *Observation of B's Lesson on Overhead Transparencies.* Unpublished report, University of Georgia, Apr. 30, 1987.

Brent, E. "Qualitative Computing: Approaches and Issues." *Qualitative Sociology*, 1984, 7 (1 and 2), 34–60.

Bromley, D. B. *The Case-Study Method in Psychology and Related Disciplines.* New York: Wiley, 1986.

Burgess, R. G. (ed.). *Field Research: A Source Book and Field Manual.* London: Allen & Unwin, 1982.

Burlingame, M., and Geske, T. G. "State Politics and Education: An Examination of Selected Multiple-State Case Studies." *Educational Administration Quarterly*, 1979, *15* (2), 50–75.

Burnett, J. *Useful Toil.* Harmondsworth: Penguin, 1977.

Cassell, J. "Risk and Benefit to Subjects of Fieldwork." *American Sociologist*, 1978, *13* (3), 134–143.

Cassell, J. "Does Risk-Benefit Analysis Apply to Moral Evaluation of Social Research?" In T. L. Beauchamp, R. R. Faden, R. J. Wallace, Jr., and L. Walters (eds.), *Ethical Issues in Social Science Research.* Baltimore: Johns Hopkins University Press, 1982.

Chein, I. "Appendix: An Introduction to Sampling." In L. H. Kidder (ed.), *Selltiz, Wrightsman & Cook's Research Methods in Social Relations.* (4th ed.) New York: Holt, Rinehart & Winston, 1981.

Clark, G. K. *The Critical Historian.* Portsmouth, N.H.: Heinemann Educational Books, 1967.

Coles, R. *Children of Crisis.* Boston: Little, Brown, 1967.

Collins, T. S., and Noblit, G. W. *Stratification and Resegregation: The Case of Crossover High School, Memphis, Tennessee.* Memphis: Memphis State University, 1978. (ED 157 954)

Conrad, P., and Reinharz, S. "Computers and Qualitative Data: Editors' Introductory Essay." *Qualitative Sociology*, 1984, 7 (1 and 2), 3–15.

Cooper, H. M. *The Integrative Research Review: A Systematic Approach.* Newbury Park, Calif.: Sage, 1984.

Cronbach, L. J. "Beyond the Two Disciplines of Scientific Psychology." *American Psychologist*, 1975, *30*, 116–127.

Cronbach, L. J. "Prudent Aspirations for Social Inquiry." In W. H. Kruskal (ed.), *The Social Sciences: Their Nature and Uses.* Chicago: University of Chicago Press, 1982.

Dean, J. P., and Whyte, W. F. "What Kind of Truth Do You

Get?" In L. A. Dexter (ed.), *Elite and Specialized Interviewing.* Evanston, Ill.: Northwestern University Press, 1970.

Denzin, N. K. *The Research Act: A Theoretical Introduction to Sociological Methods.* Chicago: Aldine, 1970.

Dewey, J. *How We Think.* Lexington, Mass.: Heath, 1933.

Dexter, L. A. *Elite and Specialized Interviewing.* Evanston, Ill.: Northwestern University Press, 1970.

Diener, E., and Crandall, R. *Ethics in Social and Behavioral Research.* Chicago: University of Chicago Press, 1978.

Dominick, J., and Cervero, R. "A Case Study of a Problem-Solving Workshop for Northeast Georgia Health Districts." Unpublished paper, Department of Adult Education, University of Georgia, 1987.

Driessen, J. J., and Pyfer, J. "An Unconventional Setting for a Conventional Occasion: A Case Study of an Experimental Adult Educational Program." *Sociology of Education,* 1975, *48,* 111–125.

Druss, K. A. "The Analysis of Qualitative Data: A Computer Program." *Urban Life,* 1980, *9,* 332–353.

Dukes, W. F. "$N = 1$." *Psychological Bulletin,* 1965, *64,* 75–79.

Eckstein, H. "Case Study and Theory in Political Science." In F. I. Greenstein and N. W. Polsby (eds.), *Strategies of Inquiry.* Reading, Mass.: Addison-Wesley, 1975.

Eisner, E. W. "On the Differences Between Scientific and Artistic Approaches to Qualitative Research." *Educational Researcher,* 1981, *10* (4), 5–9.

Elbaz, F. "The Teacher's 'Practical Knowledge': Report of a Case Study." *Curriculum Inquiry,* 1981, *11* (1), 43–71.

Elbaz, F. *Teacher Thinking: A Study of Practical Knowledge.* London: Croom Helm; New York: Nichols, 1983.

Erickson, F. "What Makes School Ethnography 'Ethnographic'?" *Anthropology and Education Quarterly,* 1973, *4* (2), 10–19.

Erickson, F. "Qualitative Methods in Research on Teaching." In M. C. Whittrock (ed.), *Handbook of Research on Teaching.* (3rd ed.) New York: Macmillan, 1986.

Fellenz, R. A., and Conti, G. J. "Manipulating Qualitative Data with a Data Management System or Replacing the Shoe Box with the Microcomputer." In R. Zellner, J. Denton, M. Burger, and R. Kansky (eds.), *Technology in Education: Implications and Applications.* College Station: Instructional Research Laboratory, College of Education, Texas A & M University, 1987.

Firestone, W. A. "Meaning in Method: The Rhetoric of Quantitative and Qualitative Research." *Educational Researcher,* 1987, *16* (7), 16–21.

Firestone, W. A., and Herriott, R. E. "Multisite Qualitative Policy Research: Some Design and Implementation Issues." In D. M. Fetterman (ed.), *Ethnography in Educational Evaluation.* Newbury Park, Calif.: Sage, 1984.

Foreman, P. B. "The Theory of Case Studies." *Social Forces,* 1948, *26* (4), 408–419.

Frankenberg, R. "Participant Observers." In R. G. Burgess (ed.), *Field Research: A Sourcebook and Field Manual.* London: Allen & Unwin, 1982.

Freidheim, E. A. "Field Research and Word Processor Files: A Technical Note." *Qualitative Sociology,* 1984, 7 (1 and 2), 90–97.

Gans, H. J. "The Participant Observer as a Human Being: Observations on the Personal Aspects of Fieldwork." In R. G. Burgess (ed.), *Field Research: A Sourcebook and Field Manual.* London: Allen & Unwin, 1982.

Gassaway, B. M., Elder, W. L., and Campbell, J. "Word Processors for Qualitative Sociologists: A Review Essay." *Qualitative Sociology,* 1984, 7 (1 and 2), 157–168.

George, A. L. "Case Studies and Theory Development: The Method of Structured, Focused Comparison." In P. G. Lauren (ed.), *Diplomacy: New Approaches in History, Theory, and Policy.* New York: Free Press, 1979.

Gerson, E. M. "Qualitative Research and the Computer." *Qualitative Sociology,* 1984, 7 (1 and 2), 61–75.

Gillespie, G. W., Jr. "Using Word Processor Macros for Computer-Assisted Qualitative Analysis." *Qualitative Sociology,* 1986, *9* (3), 283–292.

Glaser, B. G. *Theoretical Sensitivity.* Mill Valley, Calif.: Sociology Press, 1978.

Glaser, B. G., and Strauss, A. L. *The Discovery of Grounded Theory.* Chicago: Aldine, 1967.

Goetz, J. P., and LeCompte, M. D. *Ethnography and Qualitative Design in Educational Research.* Orlando, Fla.: Academic Press, 1984.

Good, C., and Scates, D. *Methods of Research.* East Norwalk, Conn.: Appleton-Century-Crofts, 1954.

Guba, E. G. *Toward a Methodology of Naturalistic Inquiry in Educational Evaluation.* Monograph Series no. 8. Los Angeles: Center for the Study of Evaluation, University of California, 1978.

Guba, E. G. "What Have We Learned About Naturalistic Evaluation?" *Evaluation Practice,* 1987, *8* (1), 23–43.

Guba, E. G., and Lincoln, Y. S. *Effective Evaluation.* San Francisco: Jossey-Bass, 1981.

Halfpenny, P. "The Analysis of Qualitative Data." *Sociological Review,* 1979, *27,* 799–825.

Hammersley, M., Scarth, J., and Webb, S. "Developing and Testing Theory: The Case of Research on Pupil Learning and Examinations." In R. G. Burgess (ed.), *Issues in Educational Research: Qualitative Methods.* London: Falmer Press, 1985.

Hardin, P. "Generativity in Middle Adulthood." Unpublished doctoral dissertation, Department of Leadership and Educational Policy Studies, Northern Illinois University, 1985.

Hawkins, R. P. "Developing a Behavior Code." In D. P. Hartmann (ed.), *Using Observers to Study Behavior.* New Directions for Methodology of Social and Behavioral Science, no. 14. San Francisco: Jossey-Bass, 1982.

Helmstadter, G. C. *Research Concepts in Human Behavior.* East Norwalk, Conn.: Appleton-Century-Crofts, 1970.

Hoaglin, D. C., and others. *Data for Decisions.* Cambridge, Mass.: Abt, 1982.

Holsti, O. R. *Content Analysis for the Social Sciences and Humanities.* Reading, Mass.: Addison-Wesley, 1969.

Honigmann, J. J. "Sampling in Ethnographic Fieldwork." In R. G. Burgess (ed.), *Field Research: A Sourcebook and Field Manual.* London: Allen & Unwin, 1982.

Houle, C. O. *Patterns of Learning: New Perspectives on Life-Span Education.* San Francisco: Jossey-Bass, 1984.

Imber, S. D., and others. "Ethical Issues in Psychotherapy Research: Problems in a Collaborative Clinical Trials Study."

American Psychologist, 1986, *41* (2), 137–146.

Jacob, E. "Qualitative Research Traditions: A Review." *Review of Educational Research*, 1987, *57* (1), 1–50.

Jacob, E. "Clarifying Qualitative Research: A Focus on Tradition." *Educational Researcher*, 1988, *17*, 16–19, 22–24.

James, P. "The Study of Educational Policy Making: A Critique of the Case Study Method." *Educational Administration*, 1981, *9* (3), 80–89.

Jarvie, I. C. "The Problem of Ethical Integrity in Participant Observation." In R. G. Burgess (ed.), *Field Research: A Sourcebook and Field Manual.* London: Allen & Unwin, 1982.

Junker, B. H. *Field Work: An Introduction to the Social Sciences.* Chicago: University of Chicago Press, 1960.

Kaplan, A. *The Conduct of Inquiry: Methodology for Behavioral Science.* San Francisco: Chandler, 1964.

Katz, J. "A Theory of Qualitative Methodology: The Social Science System of Analytic Fieldwork." In R. M. Emerson (ed.), *Contemporary Field Research.* Boston: Little, Brown, 1983.

Kazdin, A. E. "Observer Effects: Reactivity of Direct Observation." In D. P. Hartmann (ed.), *Using Observers to Study Behavior.* New Directions for Methodology of Social and Behavioral Science, no. 14. San Francisco: Jossey-Bass, 1982.

Kelman, H. C. "Ethical Issues in Different Social Science Methods." In T. L. Beauchamp, R. R. Faden, R. J. Wallace, Jr., and L. Walters (eds.), *Ethical Issues in Social Science Research.* Baltimore: Johns Hopkins University Press, 1982.

Kemmis, S. "The Imagination of the Case and the Invention of the Study." In *Case Study: An Overview.* Case Study Methods 1 (Series). Victoria, Australia: Deakin University Press, 1983.

Kennedy, M. M. "Generalizing from Single Case Studies." *Evaluation Quarterly*, 1979, *3*, 661–679.

Kenny, W. R., and Grotelueschen, A. D. *Making the Case for Case Study.* Occasional Paper, Office for the Study of Continuing Professional Education. Urbana-Champaign: College of Education, University of Illinois, 1980.

Kerlinger, F. N. *Foundations of Behavioral Research.* (3rd. ed.) New York: Holt, Rinehart & Winston, 1986.

Kidder, L. H. "Qualitative Research and Quasi-Experimental Frameworks." In M. B. Brewer and B. E. Collins (eds.), *Scientific Inquiry and the Social Sciences*. San Francisco: Jossey-Bass, 1981a.

Kidder, L. H. *Selltiz, Wrightsman & Cook's Research Methods in Social Relations*. (4th ed.) New York: Holt, Rinehart & Winston, 1981b.

Kidder, L. H., and Fine, M. "Qualitative and Quantitative Methods: When Stories Converge." In M. M. Mark and R. L. Shotland (eds.), *Multiple Methods in Program Evaluation*. New Directions for Program Evaluation, no. 35. San Francisco: Jossey-Bass, 1987.

Kirk, J., and Miller, M. L. *Reliability and Validity in Qualitative Research*. Qualitative Research Methods Series. Vol. 1. Newbury Park, Calif.: Sage, 1986.

Kline, B. "A Case Study of a Return-to-Industry Program: An Inservice Approach for Vocational Instructors at a Two-Year Post-Secondary Institution." Unpublished doctoral dissertation, Department of Vocational Education, Virginia Polytechnic Institute and State University, 1981.

Knowles, M. S., and Associates. *Andragogy in Action: Applying Modern Principles of Adult Learning*. San Francisco: Jossey-Bass, 1984.

Leininger, M. "Nature, Rationale, and Importance of Qualitative Research Methods in Nursing." In M. Leininger (ed.), *Qualitative Research Methods in Nursing*. Orlando, Fla.: Grune & Stratton, 1985.

Levinson, D. J., and others. *The Seasons of a Man's Life*. New York: Knopf, 1978.

Lightfoot, S. L. *The Good High School*. New York: Basic Books, 1983.

Lijphart, A. "Comparative Politics and the Comparative Method." *American Political Science Review,* 1971, *65,* 682–694.

Lincoln, Y. S., and Guba, E. G. *Naturalistic Inquiry*. Newbury Park, Calif.: Sage, 1985.

Lofland, J. *Analyzing Social Settings: A Guide to Qualitative Observation and Analysis*. Belmont, Calif.: Wadsworth, 1971.

Lofland, J. "Styles of Reporting Qualitative Field Research."
   American Sociologist, 1974, *9*, 101–111.
Lyman, P. "Reading, Writing, and Word Processing: Toward a
   Phenomenology of the Computer Age." *Qualitative Sociol-
   ogy*, 1984, 7 (1 and 2), 75–89.
MacDonald, B., and Walker, R. "Case Study and the Social Phi-
   losophy of Educational Research." In D. Hamilton and oth-
   ers (eds.), *Beyond the Numbers Game*. London: Macmillan
   Education, 1977.
McMillan, J. H., and Schumacher, S. *Research in Education*.
   Boston: Little, Brown, 1984.
MacNeil, P. "The Dynamics of Adult Education Growth in
   Community Colleges." Unpublished doctoral dissertation,
   Department of Educational Administration, Supervision, and
   Adult Education, Rutgers University, 1981.
Malcolm, C., and Welch, W. "Case Study Evaluations: A Case in
   Point." In W. W. Welsh (ed.), *Case Study Methodology in Edu-
   cational Evaluation*. Proceedings of the 1981 Minnesota Eval-
   uation Conference. Minneapolis: Minnesota Research and
   Evaluation Center, 1981.
Mathison, S. "Why Triangulate?" *Educational Researcher*, 1988,
   17, 13–17.
Medina, M. P. "Adult Literacy in a Rural Setting: A Family
   Case Study of Literacy Use and Meaning." Unpublished doc-
   toral dissertation, Department of Educational Leadership,
   Florida State University, 1987.
Merriam, S. B. *Coping with Male Mid-Life: A Systematic Analy-
   sis Using Literature as a Data Source*. Washington, D.C.: Uni-
   versity Press, 1980.
Merriam, S. B. *Adult Development: Implications for Adult Edu-
   cation*. Information Series no. 282. Columbus, Ohio: Educa-
   tional Resources Information Center, 1984.
Merriam, S. B., and Simpson, E. L. *A Guide to Research for
   Educators and Trainers of Adults*. Malabar, Fla.: Robert E.
   Krieger Publishing Company, 1984.
Mezirow, J., Darkenwald, G. G., and Knox, A. B. *Last Gamble
   on Education: Dynamics of Adult Basic Education*. Washing-
   ton, D.C.: Adult Education Association of the USA, 1975.
Miles, M. B., and Huberman, A. M. *Qualitative Data Analysis: A*

Sourcebook of New Methods. Newbury Park, Calif.: Sage, 1984.

Moore, D. T. "Learning at Work: Case Studies in Non-School Education." *Anthropology and Education Quarterly,* 1986, *17* (3), 166–184.

Murdock, G. P. *Outline of World Cultures.* New Haven, Conn.: Human Relations Area Files, 1983.

Murdock, G. P., and others. *Outline of Cultural Materials.* New Haven, Conn.: Human Relations Area Files, 1982.

Neustadt, R. E., and Fineberg, H. *The Epidemic That Never Was: Policy-making and the Swine Flu Affair.* New York: Vintage, 1983.

Offerman, M. "A Case Study of Failed Consortia of Higher Education." Unpublished doctoral dissertation, Department of Leadership and Educational Policy Studies, Northern Illinois University, 1985.

Owens, R. G. "Methodological Rigor in Naturalistic Inquiry: Some Issues and Answers." *Educational Administration Quarterly,* 1982, *18* (2), 2–21.

Patton, M. Q. *Qualitative Evaluation Methods.* Newbury Park, Calif.: Sage, 1980.

Patton, M. Q. "Quality in Qualitative Research: Methodological Principles and Recent Developments." Invited address to Division J of the American Educational Research Association, Chicago, April 1985.

Posner, J. "Urban Anthropology: Fieldwork in Semifamilial Settings." In W. B. Shaffier, R. A. Stebbins, and A. Turowetz (eds.), *Fieldwork Experience.* New York: St. Martin's Press, 1980.

Punch, M. *The Politics and Ethics of Fieldwork.* Qualitative Research Methods Series. Vol. 3. Newbury Park, Calif.: Sage, 1986.

Ratcliffe, J. W. "Notions of Validity in Qualitative Research Methodology." *Knowledge: Creation, Diffusion, Utilization,* 1983, *5* (2), 147–167.

Rathje, W. L. "Trace Measures." In L. Sechrest (ed.), *Unobtrusive Measurement Today.* New Directions for Methodology of Social and Behavioral Science, no. 1. San Francisco: Jossey-Bass, 1979.

Reese, H. W., and Fremouw, W. J. "Normal and Normative Ethics in Behavioral Sciences." *American Psychologist,* 1984, *39* (8), 863–876.

Reichardt, C. S., and Cook, T. D. "Beyond Qualitative Versus Quantitative Methods." In T. D. Cook and C. S. Reichardt (eds.), *Qualitative and Quantitative Methods in Evaluation Research.* Newbury Park, Calif.: Sage, 1979.

Reid, J. B. "Observer Training in Naturalistic Research." In D. P. Hartmann (ed.), *Using Observers to Study Behavior.* New Directions for Methodology of Social and Behavioral Science, no. 14. San Francisco: Jossey-Bass, 1982.

Reinharz, S. *On Becoming a Social Scientist: From Survey Research and Participant Observation to Experiential Analysis.* San Francisco: Jossey-Bass, 1979.

Riley, M. W. *Sociological Research.* Vol. 1: *A Case Approach.* San Diego: Harcourt Brace Jovanovich, 1963.

Rist, R. C. "On the Application of Ethnographic Inquiry to Education: Procedures and Possibilities." *Journal of Research in Science Teaching,* 1982, *19,* 439–450.

Rosenfeldt, A. B. "Faculty Commitment to the Improvement of Teaching Via Workshop Participation." Unpublished doctoral dissertation, Department of Vocational Education, Virginia Polytechnic Institute and State University, 1981.

Rubin, L. B. *Just Friends: The Role of Friendship in Our Lives.* New York: Harper & Row, 1985.

Rudduck, J. "A Study in the Dissemination of Action Research." In R. G. Burgess (ed.), *The Research Process in Educational Settings: Ten Case Studies.* London: Falmer Press, 1984.

Sanders, J. R. "Case Study Methodology: A Critique." In W. W. Welsh (ed.), *Case Study Methodology in Educational Evaluation.* Proceedings of the 1981 Minnesota Evaluation Conference. Minneapolis: Minnesota Research and Evaluation Center, 1981.

Schatzman, L., and Strauss, A. L. *Field Research.* Englewood Cliffs, N.J.: Prentice-Hall, 1973.

Scriven, M. "Objectivity and Subjectivity in Educational Research." In L. G. Thomas (ed.), *Philosophical Redirection of*

Educational Research: The Seventy-First Yearbook of the National Society for the Study of Education. Chicago: University of Chicago Press, 1972.

Seidel, J. V., and Clark, J. A. "The Ethnograph: A Computer Program for the Analysis of Qualitative Data." *Qualitative Sociology,* 1984, 7 (1 and 2), 110–125.

Selltiz, C., Jahoda, M., Deutsch, M., and Cook, S. W. *Research Methods in Social Relations.* New York: Holt, Rinehart & Winston, 1959.

Shaw, K. E. "Understanding the Curriculum: The Approach Through Case Studies." *Journal of Curriculum Studies,* 1978, *10* (1), 1–17.

Sieber, S. D. "The Integration of Fieldwork and Survey Methods." In R. G. Burgess (ed.), *Field Research: A Source Book and Field Manual.* London: Allen & Unwin, 1982.

Smith, A. G., and Louis, K. S. (eds.). "Multimethod Policy Research: Issues and Applications." *American Behavioral Scientist,* 1982, *26* (1), 1–144.

Smith, J. K., and Heshusius, L. "Closing Down the Conversation: The End of the Quantitative–Qualitative Debate." *Educational Researcher,* 1986, *15* (1), 4–13.

Smith, L. M. "An Evolving Logic of Participant Observation, Educational Ethnography and Other Case Studies." In L. Shulman (ed.), *Review of Research in Education.* Chicago: Peacock, 1978.

Spradley, J. P. *The Ethnographic Interview.* New York: Holt, Rinehart & Winston, 1979.

Spradley, J. P. *Participant Observation.* New York: Holt, Rinehart & Winston, 1980.

Stake, R. E. "The Case Study Method in Social Inquiry." *Educational Researcher,* 1978, 7, 5–8.

Stake, R. E. "Case Study Methodology: An Epistemological Advocacy." In W. W. Welsh (ed.), *Case Study Methodology in Educational Evaluation.* Proceedings of the 1981 Minnesota Evaluation Conference. Minneapolis: Minnesota Research and Evaluation Center, 1981.

Stenhouse, L. "Case Study and Case Records: Towards a Contemporary History of Education." *British Educational Re-*

search Journal, 1978, *4* (2), 21–39.

Stone, P. J., Dunphy, D. C., Smith, M. S., and Ogilvie, D. M. *The General Inquirer: A Computer Approach to Content Analysis.* Cambridge, Mass.: MIT Press, 1966.

Strauss, A. L. *Qualitative Analysis for Social Scientists.* Cambridge, England: Cambridge University Press, 1987.

Strauss, A., Schatzman, L., Bucher, R., and Sabshin, M. *Psychiatric Ideologies and Institutions.* (2nd ed.) New Brunswick, N.J.: Transaction Books, 1981.

Swisher, K. "Authentic Research: An Interview on the Way to the Ponderosa." *Anthropology & Education Quarterly,* 1986, *17,* 185–188.

Taylor, S. J., and Bogdan, R. *Introduction to Qualitative Research Methods.* (2nd ed.) New York: Wiley, 1984.

Tesch, R. Qualitative Research Management, 112 Mohawk Road, P.O. Box 30070, Santa Barbara, CA 93130, May 1986.

Vaillant, G. E. *Adaptation to Life.* Boston: Little, Brown, 1977.

Van Dalen, D. B. *Understanding Educational Research.* New York: McGraw-Hill, 1966.

Walker, R. "The Conduct of Educational Case Studies: Ethics, Theory and Procedures." In W. B. Dockerell and D. Hamilton (eds.), *Rethinking Educational Research.* London: Hodder & Stoughton, 1980.

Webb, E. T., and others. *Unobtrusive Measures.* Skokie, Ill.: Rand McNally, 1966.

Webb, E. T., and others. *Nonreactive Measures in the Social Sciences.* Boston: Houghton Mifflin, 1981.

Weber, R. P. "Computer-Aided Content Analysis: A Short Primer." *Qualitative Sociology,* 1984, *7* (1 and 2), 126–147.

Werner, O., and Schoepfle, G. M. *Systematic Fieldwork: Ethnographic Analysis and Data Management.* Vol. 2. Newbury Park, Calif.: Sage, 1987.

Whyte, W. F. "Interviewing in Field Research." In R. G. Burgess (ed.), *Field Research: A Source Book and Field Manual.* London: Allen & Unwin, 1982.

Wilson, S. "Explorations of the Usefulness of Case Study Evaluations." *Evaluation Quarterly,* 1979, *3,* 446–459.

Wolcott, H. "How to Look Like an Anthropologist Without

Really Being One." *Practicing Anthropology,* 1980, *3* (2), 6–7, 56–59.

Woods, P. "New Songs Played Skillfully: Creativity and Technique in Writing Up Qualitative Research." In R. G. Burgess (ed.), *Issues in Educational Research: Qualitative Methods.* London: Falmer Press, 1985.

Yin, R. K. *Case Study Research: Design and Methods.* Newbury Park, Calif.: Sage, 1984.

INDEX

221